ST. THÉRÈSE OF LISIEUX SPOUSE AND VICTIM

The Itinerary of Grace at Work in her Soul
from Baptism To Spiritual Marriage
and Self-Offering

D1603757

Cliff Ermatinger

ICS Publications
Institute of Carmelite Studies
Washington, D.C.
2010

ICS Publications
2131 Lincoln Road, NE
Washington, DC 20002-1199

www.icspublications.org

Typeset and produced in the United States of America

Library of Congress Cataloging-in-Publication Data

Ermatinger, Cliff
St. Thérèse of Lisieux, spouse and victim : the itinerary of grace at
work in her soul from baptism to spiritual marriage and self-offering /
Cliff Ermatinger.
    p. cm.
Includes bibliographical references (pp. 121–123).
ISBN 978-0-935216-78-3
    1. Thérèse, de Lisieux, Saint, 1873–1897. 2 Christian saints—France—
Lisieux—Biography. 3. Lisieux (France)—Biography. I. Title. II. Title:
Saint Thérèse of Lisieux, spouse and victim.
BX4700.T5E69 2010
282.092—dc22
    [B]
                                        2010001665

Contents

God has put her to the test and found her worthy to be with him; he has tested her like gold in a furnace, and accepted her as a holocaust.

—Cf. Wis. 3:5

Introduction

God's grace was especially active on Christmas night, 1886, in France. At the same time Paul Claudel entered Notre Dame Cathedral with the intention of meeting someone who never arrived and found Someone else was there awaiting him with graces of conversion, something similar happened in a nearby church around that same time. A soldier, burnt out from reckless living, wandered into a confessional almost unawares. He had not planned on going into a church, much less into a confessional. But one confession on top of a life of debauchery was enough to free Charles de Foucauld from his slavery to vice. Leaving the old man of sin behind him, he went on to live the life of the New Man in Christ as a modern desert father.

On that same Christmas eve, not very far away, a young girl received her portion of grace. Although it was the littleness of the Christ Child that reached out to this girl and taught her to be forever like a child, the grace was by no means small. Her long bout with scruples and empty fears was over and, in her own words, "since that night I have never been defeated in any combat, but rather walked from victory to victory."[1]

With the help of God's grace, Thérèse Martin was freed from psychological fragility "in one instant."[2] More than that, she also "felt charity enter into [her] soul"[3] which inundated her with such love for Christ and souls that from that moment onwards, apostolic zeal would supersede every personal interest. Such was her experience of God's mercy that she decided then and there to give her life over to the mission of the conversion of sinners.

This little book treats of a love story that began on January 4, 1873, Thérèse's baptism. On that day God began to court the soul of this little girl who would remain just that—a little girl. She would also learn to correspond with her baptismal grace, thus maturing into a strong—willed woman and, ultimately, the faithful bride of her divine Spouse.

St. Thomas Aquinas[4] wrote that "the first thing that is necessary for every Christian is faith, without which no one is truly called a faithful Christian. Faith brings about four good effects. The first is that through faith the soul is united to God, and by it there is between the soul and God a union akin to marriage. 'I will espouse thee in faith.' "[5]

In other words, that Thérèse Martin should become St. Thérèse, a bride of Christ, should only appear logical to us in light of St. Thomas' doctrine. If espousal with God is the fruit of the act of faith, then this must also be a universal vocation and not something exclusive to consecrated souls. God's courtship of the soul begins in baptism. Certainly, the nature of love is that it must be freely offered and the response must also be given in freedom, but often God's proposal is left unrequited—hence, the scandal of sin. But when his offer is accepted whole-heartedly and with the radical response demanded of an authentic act of faith, then the soul enters into a marital covenant with God and takes upon itself all the dignity and privileges accorded to this state.

This faithful matrimonial love implies total participation in the life of one's spouse, experiencing in one's own soul the spouse's interior and exterior trials. Naturally, St. Thérèse of Lisieux, faithful spouse to Christ, could do no less than offer herself together with her divine Spouse as an expiatory victim soul for the salvation of sinners.

Her formal relationship with Christ and her new insertion into his life began fittingly on Christmas. Also fittingly, her relationship with him on earth would end on Calvary.

Between Bethlehem and Calvary, St. Thérèse of Lisieux would share in her Spouse's joys, sorrows, trials and always his peace. Further, like her Spouse, she could not remain indifferent to his rejection by so many souls. Her relationship with these souls began under the auspices of maternal love and intercession. It would transform with time into fraternal love and solidarity—and the vicarious suffering to which both loves expose themselves.

Tracing St. Thérèse of Lisieux's life, we discover a pattern of growth which follows a six stage vocational trajectory. She begins with the life of grace, going from child of God to child in the Son. She then advances to a theological existence; from theological existence to union; and from union to its culmination in espousals with Christ: the ordinary *terminus* of the spiritual life to which everyone is called. Only the mystics arrive at spiritual marriage in this life. Having arrived at such union with the divine Spouse, the mystic is then inducted into the victimhood of Christ. Then we will then examine the relation between the type of victimhood St. Thérèse experienced with the type of sin she was expiating: namely, atheism.

The first part of the chapters that trace St. Thérèse's spiritual itinerary follow a pattern which lays down the theological foundation for each step of her journey based on patristic and Thomistic statements on grace. These, in turn, are illustrated by the saint's own writings regarding that stage in her life in the second part of those chapters. The somewhat dense theological statements find simple exemplification thanks to Thérèse's ability to express her experience of "lived theology."[6]

PART I

St. Thérèse's Life and Theology

Now I rejoice in my sufferings for your sake, and in my flesh I complete what is lacking in Christ's afflictions for the sake of his body, the Church.

—*Col. 1:24*

Chapter 1

A Snapshot of the Saint's Life

Everything on this earth smiled on me

Two days after her birth on January 2, 1873, Louis Martin and Zélie Guérin baptised their daughter Marie-Francoise-Thérèse in Alencon, France. This first phase of her life was a time when "everything on this earth smiled on me," using her own words. In her autobiography, she recalls how she used to hide behind curtains so as not to be discovered and, therefore, "be alone with God." Amongst her first memories was her prodigious decision to become a religious. True, she manifested this desire when it was said that her favourite sister would most likely become a nun and such words from a child might not be taken seriously. But the fact is that she stayed true to this decision until her painful and drawn out death. She says:

> This is one of my first memories and I haven't changed my resolution since then! It was through you dear Mother,[1] that

Jesus chose to espouse me to Himself. You were not with me then, but already a bond was formed between our souls. You were my *ideal*; I wanted to be like you, and it was your example that drew me toward the Spouse of Virgins at the age of two.[2]

Already she sensed a vocation to divine nuptials—the universal vocation rarely fulfilled in this life.

Darkness looms

At four and half years of age, Thérèse lost her mother, an event which had profound effects on Thérèse's psychology. The entire family, consisting of Louis and his five daughters, moved to Lisieux to start life anew. This second phase lasted nine years. Severely affected by the death of her mother, Thérèse called this period her most painful. She suffered abnormal timidity and became withdrawn and morose. Her proclivity to tears and hyper-sensitivity turned into hysteria when her older sister, Pauline, whom Thérèse had taken for her "second mother" unexpectedly joined the Discalced Carmelites of Lisieux. She spent the next two months thrashing about in her bed, banging her head on the bedposts, afflicted by terrifying hallucinations. Late in her short life she would attribute the cause to nothing less than satanic influences on her soul.[3] Her distraught family turned to the Blessed Virgin for assistance and the hysteria came immediately to a halt on the 13th of May, 1883, the Solemnity of Pentecost.

Shortly after bounding that hurdle—with the help of what her family considered a miracle of the Blessed Virgin—she began her preparation for First Holy Communion. One year later, while on retreat, she fell into a crisis and found herself plagued by obsessive scrupulosity. This period would last for a year and a half. During this time, her older sister Marie proved a balanced counsellor and a source of stability for the neurotic Thérèse. But when Marie decided unexpectedly to enter Carmel too, Thérèse felt herself orphaned a third time. With nowhere to turn, she sought aid from her four brothers and sisters who had preceded her entry into heaven with the confidence that they were obliged to help their youngest sister. She did not have to wait long to be liberated from her neurosis. Nonetheless, her sentimental swings and all too frequent tears and pouting would prove a cross for her family, above all for her father who simply sought new ways to make her happy.

From the moment of her decision until her entrance into Carmel at the age of 15 years, her life was a test of patience and confidence in God's Providence. In the meantime, her diocese organized a pilgrimage to Rome and Thérèse saw this as her opportunity to ask Pope Leo XIII the special permission she needed to enter Carmel at such a young age. On that trip, Thérèse seems to have had a brush with the object of her life's mission. The register of the hotel where the Martins stayed reveals that they shared the hotel with Friedrich Nietzsche, the father of nihilism[4]—Europe's newest and most deadly malady. Thérèse Martin and Friedrich Nietzsche would meet years later on a spiritual battle field on both sides of this modern drama. Benedict XV called St. Thérèse the saint with a "new mission" who offered a "new model of sanctity."[5] This new model of sanctity also underwent the greatest of modern trials—the temptation to nihilism.

Suffering opened wide its arms to me

Eventually she received the necessary permission to enter the convent and wrote: "I felt that Carmel was the desert where God wanted me to go to hide. I felt so much force that there wasn't the least doubt in my heart."[6] It is important to understand that this was not the fruit of sentiments or emotions or psychological pressure, and certainly nothing like a *fuga mundi*. Thérèse goes on to say "It was not the dream of a child led astray but the certitude of a divine call; I wanted to go to Carmel not for Pauline's sake but for Jesus' alone. I was thinking very much about things that words could not express but which left a great peace in my soul."[7]

St. Thérèse describes her entrance into Carmel: "suffering opened wide its arms to me and I threw myself into them with love."[8] Shortly after formally turning her back on the secular world as she embraced the world in need of Christ, she began to feel the weight of his cross. Her father, who had joyfully seen his last daughter depart for the religious life began to bear his own cross in the form of a painful and humiliating illness which would commit him to an insane asylum. Voices within and without the convent could be heard referring to the Martin sisters "the daughters of the crazy man."[9]

Divine nuptials

On September 8, 1890, Thérèse celebrated her long awaited spiritual wedding with the King of kings in the guise of her first Profession. That day she was more determined than ever to become "a great saint."[10] She lived her religious life with meticulous and loving fidelity, seeing in prayer, sacrifice, obedience and apostolic zeal the only expressions of matrimonial love worthy of her Spouse. Five years later her mission would intensify. With the permission of her superior, she offered herself as a victim of holocaust to the merciful Love of God in order to win back those in the darkness of unbelief. Within five days, Thérèse received a mystical wound of love in her heart as she prayed her *via crucis*, proof to her that God had accepted her oblation. Seven and a half years of religious life were enough to bring to perfection her vocation as spouse of Christ and her earthly mission as victim soul for the salvation of atheists. During the last sixteen months, the young woman heroically endured the effects of tuberculosis concomitantly with a much worse interior trial which sounded the depths of her faith and hope. Minutes before her death, she raised her wasted away and long immobile body, and her eyes looked like flames as she gazed lovingly at Someone the other sisters could not see. Her sallow and pale face became rejuvenated and she gasped "My God, I love you," and died in ecstasy. In the end, Thérèse succumbed to suffocation, much like her beloved crucified Spouse. And in that same instant, he welcomed his faithful bride into his definitive and eternal embrace for which they both had longed.

Out of his infinite glory, may he give you the Power
through his Spirit for your hidden self to grow strong,
So that Christ may live in your hearts through faith, and
then, Planted in love and built on love, you will with all
the saints Have strength to grasp the breadth and the
length, the height and the depth; until knowing the love
of Christ, which is Beyond all knowing, you are filled
with the utter fullness of God.

—*Eph. 3:14–19*

Chapter 2

The Science of Love

The works of a doctor of the Church

Not long before her death, she overheard some other nuns
speaking about having almost nothing to say about her in her
soon to be published obituary. No doubt she chuckled at the
observation. She relished such opportunities to disappear in
order to be all for Christ and have him all for herself. Some
of her sisters though, already surmised that they had a saint
on their hands. In the interest of the entire order, her superior
ordered her to put her autobiography to paper. It consists of
three manuscripts, A, B, and C.

Manuscript A: recollections from her childhood and
adolescence and her first experiences as a Carmelite.
It was written in 1895. (A)

10

Manuscript B: a masterpiece of ecclesiology and lived theology, it was written in September, 1896. (B)

Manuscript C: written in June of 1897, recounts her Carmelite life. (C)

Her other writings are:

Pious Recreations[1] or plays to be performed in the convent on certain feast days. (PR)

Poetry (P)

Prayers (Pr)

Letters (L)

Last Conversations, a collection of her words and counsels during the last months of her earthly life. (LC)

Her theological foundation

She lived almost half as long as her spiritual father, St. John of the Cross, the great Spanish mystic and Doctor of the Church, but produced more prose than he. Further, she wrote three times more poetry than he did. And all of her writings found their source in prayer, the intimate encounter between two loving hearts:

> "This is my prayer. I ask Jesus to draw me into the flames of His love, to unite me so closely to Him that He will live and act in me. I feel that the more the fire of love burns within my heart, the more I shall say: *"draw me,"* the more also the souls who will approach me (poor little piece of iron, useless if I withdraw from the divine furnace), the more these souls *will*

run swiftly in the odor of the ointments of their beloved, for a soul
that is burning with love cannot remain inactive."[2]

St. Thérèse reflects in her writings the experiences of a
generous follower of Christ who knew how to fulfil his commandments of love for God (Mt. 23:37), love for neighbour
(Mt. 23:39), missionary zeal (Mt. 28:19), and perfection (in
love—Mt. 5:48). All of these aspects are dimensions of one
love Thérèse had for Christ, "the one thing necessary."

The Lord's words on this point are too precise for us to
diminish their import. Many things are necessary for the
Church's journey through history, not least in this new century; but without charity (*agape*), all will be in vain. It is again
the Apostle Paul, who reminds us in the *Hymn to love*: even if
we speak the tongues of men and of angels, and if we have
faith "to move mountains," but are without love, all will come
to "nothing" (cf. 1 Cor 13:2). Love is truly the "heart" of the
Church, as was well understood by Saint Thérèse of Lisieux,
who was proclaimed a Doctor of the Church precisely because
she is an expert in the science of love:[3]

> I understood that the Church had a Heart and that this Heart
> was aflame with Love. I understood that Love alone stirred
> the members of the Church to act . . . I understood that Love
> encompassed all vocations, that Love was everything.[4]

Despite her inadequate formal training and lack of
resources for studying and interpreting Sacred Scripture,
Thérèse immersed herself in the Word of God with singular
depth. Her spontaneous and frequent references in her autobiography, letters, and other works manifest the primacy of

place the revealed Word had in her thought. Her prodigious memory enabled her to memorize Kempis' *Imitation of Christ* as well as the *Catechism*, almost word for word, both of which she referred to often.

Lived Theology

In a certain sense it can be said that her theology is more akin to the pre-scholastic symbolic theology produced by the likes of St. Bernard of Clairvaux[5] and other monks of his age. More than erudition and headiness, hers is a lived theology. This theological result happily requires the corresponding method of experience, which makes such a theologian an expert in the truest sense of the word. The Holy Father, Pope John Paul II, calls this "the lived theology of the saints."

> . . . we are greatly helped not only by theological investigation but also by that great heritage which is *the "lived theology" of the saints*. The saints offer us precious insights which enable us to understand more easily the intuition of faith, thanks to the special enlightenment which some of them have received from the Holy Spirit, or even through their personal experience of those terrible states of trial which the mystical tradition describes as the "dark night." Not infrequently the saints have undergone *something akin to Jesus' experience on the Cross* in the paradoxical blending of bliss and pain.[6]

The nature of such a theological method is metalogical whose tools of trade surpass the limits of rational discourse and finds its seat in love; for this is the theology of communion, fruit of "knowing the love of Christ, which is beyond all knowing" (Eph. 3:19). This lived theology is

> *the domain of communion* (*koinonia*), which embodies and
> reveals the very essence of the mystery of the Church. Com-
> munion is the fruit and demonstration of that love which
> springs from the heart of the Eternal Father and is poured out
> upon us through the Spirit which Jesus gives us (cf. Rom 5:5),
> to make us all "one heart and one soul" (Acts 4:32). It is in
> building this communion of love that the Church appears as
> "sacrament," as the "sign and instrument of intimate union
> with God and of the unity of the human race.[7]

The fruit of this lived theology is the science of love. It is
precisely this

> science of divine Love which the Father of mercies pours out
> through Jesus Christ in the Holy Spirit, is a gift granted to the
> little and the humble so that they may know and proclaim
> the secrets of the kingdom, hidden from the learned and the
> wise; for this reason Jesus rejoiced in the Holy Spirit, prais-
> ing the Father who graciously willed it so (cf. Lk 10:21–22;
> Mt 11:25–26).[8]

Applying the fruits of love

The Holy Father compared St. Thérèse of Lixieux to another
bride of Christ and Doctor of the Church, St. Catherine of
Sienna.[9] More than a happy coincidence, this mention under-
lines the communion aspect of lived theology. Saints always
enlighten other saints to understand the divine Beloved, his
mysteries, and the path to sanctity and its trials.[10] The com-
parison goes further. St. Catherine acted as spiritual mother
for the condemned convict, Niccoló di Toldo, and stormed

heaven for his conversion in something of a foreshadow-
ing of St. Thérèse's spiritual maternity for a condemned man
named Pranzini, whom Thérèse adopted as her own spiritual
son. Whereas St. Catherine[11] had a vision of her son's entrance
into God's embrace, St. Thérèse saw nothing supernatural
to confirm that her prayers were heard—yet trusted, "hop-
ing against all hope" (Rom. 4:18). As spiritual mothers to lost
souls, both mothers merited what their children needed but
were not capable of asking for or earning. This is only possible
through a certain communion with God, foundation of lived
theology. This is the leverage authentic spouses of God wield
thanks to their elevated degree of holiness.[12]

In contrast to the "mysteries hidden from the learned and
wise" (Mt. 12:25), the science of divine Love, fruit of lived theology, is available to those prepared to be humbled and loving.
"The nature of love is to humble oneself,"[13] said St. Thérèse in
reference to the Incarnation. Her observation applies also to
knowledge of the incarnate One: without humility and charity,
knowledge of God remains confined to the category of information. But, the Holy Father says, Mother Church rejoices

> that throughout history the Lord has continued to reveal
> himself to the little and the humble, enabling his chosen
> ones, through the Spirit who "searches everything, even the
> depths of God" (1 Cor 2:10), to speak of the gifts "bestowed
> on us by God . . . in words not taught by human wisdom
> but taught by the Spirit, interpreting spiritual truths in spiri-
> tual language" (1 Cor 2:12,13). Inexpressed with particular
> originality in her writings (cf. Ms B, 1r.). This science is the
> luminous expression of her knowledge of the mystery of

the kingdom and of her personal experience of grace. It can be considered a special charism of Gospel wisdom which Thérèse, like other saints and teachers of faith, attained in prayer (cf. Ms C, 36r.).[14]

And prayer, indeed, was her means to do theology. It took first place in her life because there she found her Beloved and knew him. Prayer was the fount of her knowledge of God to whom she called, "draw me in your footsteps, let us run" (Cant. 1:3).

All the saints have understood this, and more especially those who filled the world with the light of the Gospel teachings. Was it not in prayer that St. Paul, St. Augustine, St. John of the Cross, St. Thomas Aquinas, St. Francis, St. Dominic, and so many other famous Friends of God have drawn out this divine science which delights the greatest geniuses? A scholar has said: "*give me a lever and a fulcrum and I will lift the world.*" What Archimides was not able to obtain, for his request was not directed by God and was only made from a material viewpoint, the saints have obtained in all its fullness. The Almighty has given them a *fulcrum: HIMSELF ALONE; as* lever: Prayer which burns with a fire of love. And it is in this way that they have lifted the world; it is in this way that the saints still militant lift it, and that until the end of time, the saints will come to lift it.[15]

Symbolic theology expresses the inexpressible

To convey lived theology, Church history reveals that the mystics have had recourse to poetry to best express their experience. Often this theology is expressed in symbols. Rather than a speculative science (*fides quaerens intellectum* — "faith seeking understanding"), lived theology is a practical theology. Although the science of love is metalogical, it does not shun *scientia fidei* (the knowledge that comes from faith) or *scientia rationis* (the knowledge that comes from reason), but together with them forms a more complete knowledge of God and his mysteries. This is nothing new. Already in the 5th Century, Pseudo-Dionysius[16] presented a similar gamut of theology as made up of speculative theology, which dealt with the intelligible names of God; and symbolic theology, which treated of the sensible names of God: both interpretative tools of Sacred Scripture as Word of God, which served the highest form of theology, known as mystical theology.[17] And mystical theology is nothing if not lived theology.

Thérèse likened her heart to a lyre on whose four strings she would sing her Beloved's praises in prayer. Each string represented a perspective of her love which found expression as maternal, filial, fraternal, and spousal love.

The four dimensions of her theology could be synthesized in this fashion:

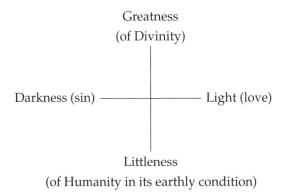

Greatness
(of Divinity)

Darkness (sin) ——————— Light (love)

Littleness
(of Humanity in its earthly condition)

The vertical line corresponds to the mystery of the Incarnation; the union without confusion between the greatness of Divinity and the littleness of Christ's sacred Humanity. The horizontal line corresponds to the Paschal mystery of redemption, the encounter between the light of divine love and the darkness of the sin of the world, taken away by Christ's death and Resurrection.

These dimensions are best understood in their contrast and in their union, made possible by the Incarnation, in which God marries our humanity; and in the redemption in which God lowers himself to the extreme of dying to save us—the proper consequence of divine Love for St. Thérèse, "since the nature of love is to humble oneself."[18]

Thérèse's theology is an expression of Incarnation and Redemption, which embraces each of the four dimensions of her beloved Spouse's earthly life and makes them her own through participation. If it is the nature of love to humble oneself, it is the nature of spousal love to participate in every aspect of the beloved's life.

A theology accessible to all

But more than symbols, St. Thérèse offers her autobiography, which is the key to understand her mind and soul. In it she speaks of the heart of what she calls "the science of love," which is divine Love, God himself, as manifested in the Sacred Heart of Jesus. The term is essentially connected with Sacred Heart devotion as found in the words Christ spoke to St. Margaret Mary Alocoque. St. Thérèse refers to *The Little Breviary of the Sacred Heart* at the beginning of her masterpiece, *Manuscript B*:

Here is the teacher whom I am giving you; he will teach you everything that you must do. I want to make you read in the book of life, wherein is contained the science of LOVE. The science of love, ah, yes, this word resounds sweetly in the ear of my soul, and I desire only this science.[19]

St. Thérèse does not offer a spiritual way made up of neatly defined stages as does her spiritual mother St. Teresa of Ávila in her *Interior Castles* or her spiritual father St. John of the Cross in his *Ascent of Mount Carmel*. Rather, hers is a simple and universal way to holiness through relentless self-giving and trust. Her trusting abandonment is reminiscent of St. Louis de Montfort, a spiritual dynamic valid for everyone. Her writings have been criticized as "subjectivist" and "intimist," but in reality her theology, as lived theology is subjective by nature. Her theology as lived theology is intimate without self-seeking. Her references to herself are solely in relation to her beloved Spouse because she is incapable of thinking of herself in any other context.

PART II

The Itinerary of Grace
in the Soul of St. Thérèse

*When we were baptised we went into the tomb with him
and joined him in death; so that as Christ was raised
from the dead by the Father's glory, we too might live a
new life in him. If in union we have imitated him in his
death, we shall also imitate him in his resurrection.*

—*Rom. 6: 4–5*

Chapter 3

*The Formal Itinerary of Grace
from Baptism to Spiritual Marriage*

The spiritual itinerary from baptism to spouse of God is not
one of linear progression but a point of encounter resulting
in an ever-deepening spiral. This fidelity to baptismal grace
means immersion in divine life which, rather enrich the soul,
strips it of what is not from God or does not lead to him, thus
bringing it to live what is called a theological existence. The
theological existence "is lived in acts which, though diverse,
spring from the same source, the grace of God; they are vivi-
fied by the very same source, the inhabitation of the Spirit;
they involve the entire person. The theological virtues are a
habitus infused in us in grace and permit reciprocal action with
divine operations. Union with him occurs in operations in

which the person in grace is the true origin."[1] Perseverance in the theological life prepares the terrain for God's transforming union, which in many cases flourishes into spiritual marriage. Thus the ordinary spiritual itinerary from baptism to spiritual marriage is the universal vocation fulfilled by all who reach heaven and experienced in this life by those persons generous enough to live in perfect consequence of their baptismal commitments.

In his *Commentary on the Sunday Sermons of the Great Fathers*, St. Thomas Aquinas compares the integral life of theological virtue to spiritual marriage with Christ:

> What, dearest brethren, are we to think He means by a wedding garment? If we say it is baptism or faith, who is there that has entered these nuptials without baptism or without faith? For whosoever is outside, it is because he has not yet believed. What then are we to understand by the wedding garment, if not charity? For whoever in the Church possesses faith, but has not charity, comes in to the wedding, but does not come in with a wedding garment. Rightly is charity called a wedding garment; for our Creator wore this upon Him when He came to the marriage of Himself with the Church. It was solely through the charity of God that His Only-Begotten joined to Himself the souls of the chosen among men. It was because of this that John says: For God so loved the world, as to give his only begotten son for us (Jn. 3:16).[2]

Spouse is every soul united to God through grace, yet quite another thing is to be chosen by God to be a victim of expiation. Such a grace is extraordinary and appears to be exclusive to those whose cooperation with grace is so single hearted that they are inducted into the experiential aspect of their spiritual nuptials in this life.

The very nature of the life of spiritual marriage includes the self-offering of oneself as a victim, since faithful spouses participate in each other's trials. In a certain sense, spiritual marriage and self-offering are existent in seed form in baptismal grace. St. Paul says:

> We are dead to sin, so how can we continue to live in it? You have been taught that when you were baptised in Christ Jesus we were baptised into his death; in other words, when we were baptised we went into the tomb with him and joined him in death; so that as Christ was raised from the dead by the Father's glory, we too might live a new life. If in union with Christ we have imitated his death, we shall also imitate him in his resurrection. We must realise that our former selves have been crucified with him to destroy this sinful body and to free us from the slavery of sin (Rom. 6:3–6).

The itinerary of grace from Thérèse's baptism until the Christmas Grace (Ms A 2r–A44r)

This period of St. Thérèse's life presents us with a soul preserved in a cocoon of Catholic spirituality. She was raised to be a prayerful person, something which came easily to her, thanks to her natural depth and proclivity to discover God in the beauty of nature or in the hours of silence in her room.

Such was St. Thérèse's understanding of the necessity of baptismal grace for salvation that she shuddered to think that she had spent thirty three hours from the time of her birth until the waters of baptism, which incorporated her into the Mystical Body of Christ, were poured over her head. Her whole life was built on the solid foundation of "water and the Spirit" (Jn. 3:5), to which she remained perfectly faithful.

Her awareness of the most profound meaning of baptism is manifest in her poetry. But of all of the effects of baptism, what predominates in her writings is the divine inhabitation in the soul of the Christian:

> Through Him, the baptismal waters
> Will make of a newborn
> The temple where God Himself
> Deigns to dwell in his Love.[3]

> But before you can see him
> One thing is needed,
> That the water of baptism spill
> Upon your soul its holy whiteness,
> That the true God may dwell there
> And the Spirit be the life of your soul.[4]

In preparation for her first confession and First Communion, she manifested her strength of will and prodigious mind by memorizing the entire Catechism.[5] Pope John Paul II writes that this "gave evidence of an extraordinary love for the truths of the faith."[6]

The garden of souls

She seemed to see herself in some children to whom she had taught catechism. They manifested the same love for the truth and an ability to make small sacrifices out of love for Christ.

She later says of children who have to come to the use of their reason:

> "Holy baptism must implant a very deep seed of the theological virtues in souls since from childhood these virtues are already evident and since the hope of future goods suffices to have them accept sacrifices. . . . Seeing innocent souls at such close range, I understand what a misfortune it was when they were not formed in their early years, when they are soft as wax upon which one can imprint either virtue or vice. I understood, too, what Jesus said: *But whoever causes one of these little ones to sin, it were better for him to have a great millstone fastened around his neck and to be thrown in the depths of the sea* (Mt. 18:6).[7]

God's grace present in the soul makes it capable of virtuous operations.

> What would happen were a clumsy gardener not to graft his bushes properly? If he was ignorant of the nature of each and wished to make roses bloom on peach trees? He's cause the tree to die, which nevertheless has been good and capable of producing fruit. It's in this way one should know from childhood what God asks of souls and second the action of His graces, without either advancing or holding back. As little birds learn to *sing* by listening to their parents, so children learn the science of the virtues, the sublime *song* of Divine Love from souls responsible for forming them.[8]

During her introspective years, she was concerned about the numbers of unbaptised in mission lands, but Christ gave her the answer in the form of a garden of souls, some wild flowers, others lilies and roses, all of whom gave God joy. More importantly, in this lesson, Christ taught her that perfection was in being what God wanted us to be.[9] This seems to be a synthesis of her thought: loving fulfilment of God's will and giving him glory by accepting it in one's own littleness.

A seed planted in the garden

Amongst the prodigies of this period is Thérèse's first memory — the desire to become a religious at the age of two. Perhaps this was the sentiment of child wanting to follow in her sister's footsteps. She admits that it might have been so. On the other hand, she also recognizes that it seems to be the means God used to call her to religious life.[10] At eight years of age, she adamantly exclaimed that "Carmel was the *desert* where God wanted her to go.[11] Between those two moments, in 1887, she had a prophetic vision in which she saw an image of her father who was away on a business trip. She saw his sickly and stooped formed, hiding its face, just as she would see him twelve years later.[12]

A pruned *Little Flower*

The time between October 2, 1882 to May 13, 1883 was turbulent for Thérèse. Pauline (Thérèse's "second mother") departed for Carmel and Thérèse felt orphaned once again. She began to have continuous headaches which culminated in a nervous breakdown. Her doctor marvelled that one so young should have such a capacity for psychological suffering. She described the illness as a sort of demonic oppression and obsession resulting in empty but constant fear and trembling with long fits in which she pounded her head against bedposts and walls. The doctors could find no cure. Unbeknownst to Thérèse, the family had a novena of Masses said for her cure. She describes the Blessed Virgin's intercession on Pentecost Day.

I was suffering very much from this forced and inexplicable struggle and Marie was suffering perhaps even more than I. After some futile attempts to show me she was by my side, Marie knelt down near my bed with Léonie and Céline. Turning to the Blessed Virgin (The image of the Lady of Victories) and praying with the fervour of a mother begging for the life of her child, Marie obtained what she wanted.

. . . All of a sudden the blessed Virgin appeared beautiful to me, so beautiful that never had I seen anything so attractive; her face was suffused with an ineffable benevolence and tenderness, but what penetrated to the very depths of my soul was the "*ravishing smile of the Virgin*." At that instant, all my pain disappeared.[13]

Thérèse admits that her hypersensitivity continued to be beyond normal, but she was capable of preserving an equally uncommon longing for God. "Since infancy," says Thérèse, her "loving and sensitive heart was oriented towards heaven and Christ,"[14] and her First Communion was a "kiss of love" and a "fusion."[15] Her theological life developed quickly and permitted her "to see Christ in everything,"[16] since "he who is joined to the Lord, is one spirit" (1 Cor. 6:17). Thus began a year of peace.

Renewed trials

Her struggle was not over, though. Thérèse attended a retreat (May 17–21, 1885) in preparation for the Anniversary of her Communion which became the occasion of her year and half long bout with the psychological malady of scruples. Finally, with nowhere else to turn, she sought liberation through intercessory prayer to her four infant siblings already enjoying the beatific vision, and was immediately cured in October, 1886. In spite of her trials and temptations to despair, Thérèse never endangered her life of grace. Later, she would recall:

> I made a general confession, something I had never made before, and at its termination he spoke the most consoling words I ever heard in my life: "*In the presence of God, the Blessed Virgin, and all the Saints, I DECLARE THAT YOU HAVE NEVER COMMITTED A MORTAL SIN.*" Then he added: "Thank God for what He has done for you; had He abandoned you, instead of being a little angel, you would have become a little demon." I had no difficulty believing it; I felt how weak and imperfect I was and gratitude flooded my soul. I had such a great fear of soiling my baptismal robe that such an assurance, coming from the mouth of my director such as St. Teresa desired, i.e., one combining *knowledge and virtue*, it seemed to me to be coming from the mouth of Jesus Himself.[17]

In short, there are three things that last: faith, hope, and love; and the greatest of these is love.

—1 Cor. 13:13

Chapter 4

Thérèse's Theological Existence

From the Christmas Grace until her Entrance in Carmel (Ms A 44v–68v)

Through baptismal grace God invades the soul. But after baptism and acquired use of reason, the believer must choose to accept and live out the consequences of this incorporation into divine life. In order to respond to grace, God infuses the human soul with the theological virtues. Faith, hope and love, "these three" (1 Cor. 13:13), sum up the soul's relationship with the one and multiform God. "If we consider the sense of Christian existence, hope is what determines it. If we consider what informs this existence, we must call it charity. If the question is asked about its foundation, we have to call it faith."[1] Just as it is God's donation of himself to the human soul which infuses the theological virtues, so too those virtues are the person's path to God. The divine indwelling forms what can be called a "new incarnation," since they permit the person to participate in his life and elevate his nature to a participation in divine nature[2] (cfr. 2 Pet. 1:4). This participation in Trinitarian life introduces the person into mutual self-giving of Father in the Son and in the Holy Spirit. Such divine operation in the soul

28

disposes the person's self-donation to the God-with-us to such an extent that it becomes one and the same offering of "I-with-God" in Jesus Christ. The Spirit of Christ is the protagonist of this action in the human soul, but not without that person's consent. And such consent is only given in the context of the many successive little self-offerings of the ascetical life: "That is why you must kill everything in you that belongs only to earthly life. . . . You have stripped off your old behaviour with your old self, and you have put on a new self which will progress towards true knowledge the more it is renewed in the image of its creator." (Col. 3:5, 9–10).

Grace unites two freedoms

In other words, more than a union of purpose, this is a union of nature (divine charity) through participation. The dynamism of such a theological existence "has God for its object: and by way of them (the theological virtues) we are correctly ordered to God; because they are infused by God alone."[3] But naming them virtues implies that their operation requires willed human acts elevated from their human potentiality by divine grace, and therefore invests the person with the responsibility to desire to be the subject of their correlative action in reciprocal rapport with God. The uninterrupted divine presence amid human cooperation brings about an ever increasing perfection in the generous and uncalculating soul to such an extent that it in-forms one's every action and reaction.

"Grace does not harm nature, it perfects it."[4] As *capax Dei* (a being capable of a rapport with God), man is made not only to encounter God, but to posses him and be possessed by him. In doing so, he reaches his perfection. All things act towards their own end, unless frustrated through abused freedom, as is the case with fallen rational creatures. Therefore, to act outside the bounds of one's *capax Dei* nature—such as through disbelief or despair—is to contradict one's own nature. Thus man's natural end is God but, his way to God (the theological virtues infused by grace) is beyond human capability, given the infinite disproportion between man and God. To actually possess grace and live according to the theological virtues requires God's direct intervention.[5] The process of human self-realization finds its consummation in a fulfilment which is infinitely beyond its reach, only because the ultimate Origin and End of this action—what one might call the metaphysical sense—are the same. Nonetheless, this metaphysical sense is precisely where human freedom resides. For it is within the context of a divine purpose, freely devised by God and freely accepted by the human person, that it comes about. Cooperation with grace is the union of two freedoms.

Taking God as his Word

The single act of faith, a human act assisted by God's grace, consists of three elements: *Deo credere, Deum credere, in Deum credere*[6] ("to believe what God says is true, to believe that he is God, and to commit oneself to God in faith"). In other words, at God's behest, the person of faith enters into a relationship of trust, a bond, a covenant with the Creator. This is not merely intellectual assent but is a radical and definitive choice for the divine Other. Therefore, John Henry Newman could say: "A person who says, 'I believe just at this moment . . . but I cannot answer for myself that I shall believe tomorrow,' does not believe."[7]

Any relationship or society is built on a type of belief or a common understanding, accepting something unconditionally as true on the testimony of someone else who understands the matter out of his own knowledge. One cannot get along in society without making hundreds of acts of "natural faith" a day. At some point, one is incapable of verifying everything and must simply make a leap of faith and trust that the pilot knows how to fly, that this bridge was well made, that the chair will support one's weight, etc. Inherent in each of these acts is a degree of trust in another person: a pilot, an architect, a carpenter. Therefore, what is required is a leap of trust whose foundation is seated in the will, since the intellect cannot reach over the abyss of unknowing. In other words, much more than an assent to an article of belief, this is an assent to the authority of the source, an assent to someone. The content of the testimony and the person of the witness are identical. In supernatural faith, God himself reveals to men the truth of heavenly mysteries and of himself: "let God Himself, who made me, teach me the mystery of heaven, not man who knew not himself. Whom rather than God should I believe concerning God?"[8]

Faith in itself is a gift, but a gift that bears within itself the responsibility to correspond with it. It binds the soul to God and brings it into a loving relationship. "We believe because we love," said Cardinal Newman.[9] As the soul's existence participates in God's existence, so too does this human act of faith participate in God's bestowing of grace. It is a response which states that the believer exists for God as it says it believes in God.

The Christmas Grace

> It was December 25, 1886, that I received the grace of leaving my childhood, in a word, the grace of my complete conversion. . . . On that night of nights began the third period of my life, the most beautiful and the most filled with graces from heaven. The work I had been unable to do in ten years was done by Jesus in one instant, contenting himself with my good will which was never lacking . . . I felt charity enter into my soul, and the need to forget myself and to please others.[10]

The period began when she was 14 years old. Thanks to what she would call her "Christmas grace," Thérèse's character changed dramatically and instantaneously; she had a maturity far beyond her years. The Christmas grace effected an authentic conversion with which she cooperated for the rest of her brief life. As a result, she overcame the emotional weakness caused by the loss of her mother and the separation from her sisters and began "to run as a giant" on the course of faith, hope, and love.[11]

I thirst

On May 29, 1887 Thérèse asked her father's permission to enter Carmel. Her vocation as spouse of Christ was decided: she would live out her vocation as a Discalced Carmelite. Shortly after revealing her intentions, a defining grace penetrated her soul while she contemplated a picture of Christ crucified. The thought that her Savior's wounds should spill blood in vain, that is, for unrepentant sinners, occasioned tremendous interior grief. Docile to that grace, she resolved to remain at the foot of the cross for the rest of her life gathering up the merits of the precious Blood in order to apply it to those very souls who scorned it. The intensity of this interior motion made her understand that this was her particular mission. From that moment until her death she heard within her heart Christ's cry *"I thirst"* (Jn. 19:28), which effected her ardent desire to slake Christ's thirst for souls by winning them for him. In particular, she intuited that her mission was to those farthest from Christ.[12] She would not have to wait long before Providence sent her the first soul entrusted to her care: the soon to be executed multiple murderer Henri Pranzini. She considered the unrepentant Pranzini to be "her first child"[13] and she spiritually showered him with maternal love. Thérèse had Masses said for his conversion and stormed heaven with her prayers and sacrifices, gathering the Blood of Christ and applying it to her newly adopted son. Although he rejected offers for a last confession, the newspaper account of his execution reported that in the last instant before his death, he turned to the nearby priest and, grabbing his crucifix, kissed the wounds of Christ three times. Although Thérèse was prepared to believe that her intercession was acceptable and effective without the least manifestation of repentance from Pranzini, his last minute gesture confirmed her of his repentance as it confirmed her in her particular mission.[14]

> I felt in the depths of my heart certain that our desires would be granted, but to obtain courage to pray for sinners I told God I was sure He would pardon the poor, unfortunate Pranzini; that I'd believe this even if he went to his death without any signs of repentance or without having gone to confession. I was absolutely confident in the mercy of Jesus.[15]

Here, we begin to see the development of her apostolic charity manifested in maternal love in all of its richness: hope, self-giving, fearlessness. Thérèse played the chord of maternal love first on her spiritual lyre.

Immediately afterwards, Thérèse reveals how this love flourishes into the total abandonment of its espousal dimension: "Passing by me, Jesus saw that the time had come to be loved, He entered into a covenant with me and I became His own."[16] Thus began the time of courtship between Thérèse and the Incarnate Word.

Because you believe, you are sure of the end

Although she advanced "from victory to victory,"[17] Thérèse never intellectualized her faith or submitted it to a rationalist litmus test. Nor did she relegate it to a certain category of her life. It became the standard for her life. Thérèse states that in spite of daily trials and seeming disappointments, her faith "was never shaken."[18] Further, she says her trials were great for her faith but

> the One whose heart watches even when he sleeps made me understand that to those whose faith is like that of a mustard seed He grants miracles and moves mountains in order to strengthen their faith which is still small [Mt. 17:19]; but for His intimate friends, for His Mother, He works no miracles before having tried their faith.[19]

This is because the test of faith is won, not by confirmation through empirical evidence measured by the intellect, but by love, measured by the will in cooperation with divine Love.

"The science of Love . . . I desire only this science,"[20] because theological love is the most authentic expression of belonging to Christ. " . . . and everyone who loves is begotten by God and knows God. Anyone who fails to love can never have known God, because God is love" (1 Jn. 4:7–8).

Thérèse's theological existence reflects the Thomistic and Juanistic teaching on the theological virtues as the soul of the spiritual life and, subsequently, of *scientia amoris*. But given what has been said with regard to primacy of charity over faith and hope, this "greatest of the them all" (cf. I Cor. 13:13) is also the most "theological." For Thérèse, Charity is "the Fire of the Fatherland"[21] which can never be extinguished. And since this earthly exile prohibits us from living "face to Face" with Christ, charity bonds us to him "heart to heart."[22] St. Thérèse lived what St. Peter wrote to the faithful:

> You did not see him, yet you love him; and still without seeing him you are already filled with the joy so glorious that it cannot be described, because you believe; and you are sure of the end to which your faith looks forward, that is, the salvation of your souls (1 Pet. 1:8).

Such was Thérèse's joy: "Jesus, my joy is to love you."[23]

Loving God with all his Heart

But what God asks of us is not simply to love him with all our heart, but through the dynamic of theological virtue, to love him with his Heart; that is, with his own divine charity present in our hearts.

Remember, that in this life all I want is to console you
For the forgetfulness of sinners you feel.
My only Love, hear my plea
To love you, you would give me a thousand hearts.
But Jesus, supreme Beauty, even that is too little
Give me your own divine Heart to love you with.
Of my burning desire, Lord,
In every moment,
Remember.[24]

This love whose source is God is the foundation and *terminus* of every vocation. This explains Christ's commandment "be perfect as your heavenly Father is perfect." (Mt. 6:48). The perfection of totality and infinity demanded from the baptised members of the Mystical Body cannot be seated in any human faculty. It must therefore find a solution in the Infinite himself. According to St. Thomas Aquinas, we can immeasurably and totally love him whom we will know perfectly only in the next life.[25] St. Thérèse confirms the Angelic Doctor's observation finding the "totality" and "infinity" in the nature of charity itself. More than pious exaggerations, Thérèse shows a keen knowledge of the mystery of theological virtue. Thus, when she writes: "I want to love him more than he has ever been loved before,"[26] she verifies what Thomas says:

For charity itself considered as such has no limit to its increase, since it is a participation of the infinite charity which is the Holy Ghost. In like manner the cause of the increase of charity, viz. God, is possessed of infinite power. Furthermore, on the part of its subject, no limit to this increase can be determined, because whenever charity increases, there is a corresponding increased ability to receive a further increase. It is therefore evident that it is not possible to fix any limits to the increase of charity in this life.[27]

*I live now not with my own life but with the life
of Christ who lives in me.*

—Gal. 2:20

Chapter 5

Thérèse's Union with Christ

(Ms A 69r–75v)

Christ who lives in me

A theological existence is a life firmly rooted in Christ. Its individual acts bring about the awareness of the divine presence in every encounter and event. A person in such a state grows exponentially as he learns to communicate with his divine Lover through the language of self-giving in fidelity and perseverance. This exponential growth depends on the degree to which one dies to oneself (*ego*) and rises with Christ, thus living the life of the Spirit of communion with Christ. The consequence is a life of union that knows no fragmentation. Hence, every thought, word, and act is part of an integral whole bound together by the presence and operation of divine love, the "bond of perfection" (Col. 3:14). The more the rapport between Christ and the person intensifies, the more that person participates in the communal "we" aspect of the theological dynamic in the soul. The nature of the act of faith, hope, and love, therefore, not only requires that it be realized in an interdependent way, but further solidifies this communal link to such an extent that it effects a fusion of persons without violating the identity of either. Rather than on a psychological level, this fusion occurs on the level of the spirit: the Spirit of Christ dwelling in the spirit. St. Paul establishes this teaching with those most radical words: "I live now not with my own life but with the life of Christ who lives in me" (Gal. 2:20).

The dynamism of the communion with the invisible Beloved, in whom faith and hope are placed,[1] is such that it seeks totality. The more one's trusting self-giving mirrors that of the Blessed Trinity, the greater the solicitude for consummation of this union.

About such a soul, St. Bernard of Clairvaux says,

The soul which has attained this degree now ventures to think of marriage. Why should she not, when she sees that she is like him and therefore ready for marriage? His loftiness has no terror for her, because her likeness to him associates her with him, and her declaration of love is a betrothal (on the Song of Songs, Vol. IV, sermon 85, no. 12, p. 208).

This prolonged spiritual communion produces the perfect man whose every faculty finds its fulfilment in God. The imperfect man thinks inordinately about himself while the perfect man continually occupies his thoughts with God, "desiring to be dissolved and to be with Christ" (Phil. 1:23).

Friendship inclines a man to wish to converse with his friend. The conversation of man with God, according to these words of St. Paul: "Our conversation is in heaven (Phil. 3:20). And as the Holy Ghost gives us the love of God, He also inclines us to contemplate Him. That is why the Apostle says: "But we all beholding the glory of the Lord with open face, are transformed into the same image from glory to glory, as by the Spirit of the Lord' " (2 Cor. 3:18; *Summa Contra Gentiles*, Bk. IV, cap. 22).

Ultimately, this person finds fulfilment in spiritual marriage. St. Paul expresses this saying that "Christ has taken (*kataleipo*) him for himself" (Phil. 3:12), which expresses an exclusive possession or relationship, the beginning of formal engagement. Thérèse's engagement was made official upon acceptance into the novitiate.

Engaged to Christ

Thérèse's time in the novitiate was a period of profound interior peace[2] which, in her words "has not even abandoned me in times of trial."[3] There "suffering opened wide its arms to me and I threw myself into them with love. I declared at the feet of Jesus-Victim, in the examination preceding my Profession, what I had come to Carmel for: "I came to save souls and especially pray for priests."[4] As the seeds of her particular mission as victim had begun to show signs of growth, so did her interior life which was blessed with union with Christ. Her novitiate was the official time of her engagement with Christ, and she used it well. Mother Agnes of Jesus (Pauline Martin), Prioress over Thérèse recalls this unitive stage in her younger sister's life:

> While she was still a novice she once spent nearly a week feeling as if she was separated from her body. "I was no longer on earth; I did my work in the refectory as if someone had

lent me a body. I just cannot express it. It was as if a veil had been thrown up between me and everything around me."[5]

Mother Agnes of Jesus had initiated Thérèse into devotion to the Holy Face, a devotion popularized in the 19th Century as devotion to the Sacred Heart flourished. The contemplation of the Face of her Beloved served to increase this union throughout her period of engagement to Christ:

> The little flower transplanted to Mount Carmel was to expand under the shadow of the cross. The tears and blood of Jesus were to be her dew, and her Sun was His adorable Face veiled with tears. Until my coming to Carmel, I had never fathomed the depths of the treasures hidden in the Holy Face. It was through you, dear Mother (Agnes), that I learned to know these treasures. Just as you had preceded us into Carmel, so also you were the first to enter deeply into the mysteries of love hidden in the Face of our Spouse . . . I desired that, like the Face of Jesus, "my face be truly hidden, that no one on earth would know me" (Is. 53:3). I thirsted after suffering and I longed to be forgotten."[6]

Later, Thérèse also confided in her Prioress the following phenomena, indication of union during that year of grace and peace:

> "In the garden during the night silence, I have often felt so deeply recollected and my heart so united with God that I used to make very intense, yet effortless, acts of love; I think these graces must have been what St. Teresa calls 'flights of the spirit.' "[7]

For growth in union her human affections as well as attachment to divine consolations had to be purified through the exercise of theological virtue. God blessed her with aridity and trial from the start. She learned that suffering silently in love not only united her to her divine Fiancée, it was also the surest means to attain her goal of saving souls. Her prioress during novitiate offered her ample opportunities to purify her love and intention. "I love Mother Prioress *very much*, but it was a pure affection which raised me to the Bridegroom of my soul."[8] And, in her own words, this love was "unto folly."

> And now I have no other desire except *to love* Jesus unto folly. My childish desires have all flown away . . . Neither do I desire any longer suffering or death, and still I love them both; it is *love* alone that attracts me, however. I desired them for a long time; I possessed suffering and believed I had touched the shores of heaven, that the little flower would be gathered in the springtime of her life. Now, abandonment alone guides me. I have no other compass. I can no longer ask for anything with fervor except the accomplishment of God's will in my soul without any creature being able to set obstacles in the way. I can speak those words of the Spiritual Canticle of Saint John of the Cross:
>
> > *In the inner wine cellar*
> > *I drank of my Beloved, and when I went abroad*
> > *Through all this valley*
> > *I no longer knew anything,*
> > *And lost the herd that I was following.*

Now I occupy my soul
And all my energy in his service;
I no longer tend the herd,
Nor have I any other work
Now that my every act is LOVE.

—*SS VIII, pp. 178–179*

*Let us be glad and joyful and give praise to God, because
this is the time for the marriage of the Lamb. His bride is
ready, and she has been able to dress herself in dazzling
white linen because her linen is made from the good
deeds of the saints.*

—*Rev 19:7–9*

The Bridegroom is here. Go out and meet him!

—*Mt. 25:6*

Chapter 6

Spiritual Marriage—First Profession

(Ms A 76r–84v)

Scriptural and Patristic Foundation
of Spiritual Marriage

The foundation of spiritual marriage is not banal poetry but
a theological reality and an expression of one's covenant of
love with Christ. Nonetheless, the concept in general does not
begin with Christianity. Jewish philosopher Philo of Alexandria taught that the soul receives the divine seed from which
are born virtues and good deeds (De cherubim 42–52; SCh.).
He echoes Plato's *Symposium* which holds that, in union with
the Beautiful, the soul engenders the virtues.

Nonetheless, the term "spiritual marriage" grates on ratio-
nalistic ears. The very fact that the term strikes moderns as

44

odd suggests the urgency with which the concept has to be revived. The concept is thoroughly scriptural, found throughout the Old Testament where God speaks of Israel in nuptial terms.[1] In the New Testament, under the New Covenant, Christ identifies himself as the divine Spouse to the Church and to individual souls, each one his bride.[2] Christianity did not have to wait long for the concept "spiritual marriage" to become a common term. Tertullian[3] writes: "when the soul comes to the Faith . . . it is received by the Holy Spirit; the flesh accompanies the soul in the spiritual marriage."[4] Origen teaches: "Christ is the spouse to whom the soul is united in faith."[5] Cyrill of Jerusalem[6] says with more precision, that after baptism, she who was a servant has received the Lord as her Spouse.[7] Dydimus the Blind[8] echoes Cyril with "he who has created our soul takes her as spouse in the baptismal fount."[9]

From Origen,[10] Gregory of Nyssa,[11] and throughout the Middle Ages into our modern era, the frequently commented *Song of Songs* provides the most explicit expression of the nuptial union between God and the human person. Perhaps St. Bernard of Clairvaux's voluminous *Sermons on the Song of Songs* best describe the process and the nature of this intimate union: *transformamur ut conformamur* (*we are transformed as we are conformed*):

> Love is sufficient for itself; when love is present it absorbs and conquers all other affections. Therefore it loves what it loves, and it knows nothing else."[12] "It is assuredly a thing most marvellous and astonishing, that likeness which accompanies the vision of God, and is itself the vision . . . Then the soul will

know as it is known and love as it is loved, and the Bridegroom will rejoice over the Bride, knowing and known, loving
and loved.[13]

Yet it would not be until St. John of the Cross, St. Thérèse
of Lisieux's spiritual father, that the intimate secrets of the internal structure of such a union would be told. In his classic work
Living Flame of Love, he says of the peak of spiritual union:

> In this matter it is worth noting the difference between the
> possession of God through grace itself and the possession of
> Him through union, for the one lies in loving, and the other
> also includes communication. The difference resembles that
> between betrothal and marriage.[14]

More precisely, he says:

> Likewise, when the soul has reached such purity in itself and
> its faculties that the will is very pure and purged of other
> alien satisfactions and appetites in the inferior and supe-
> rior parts, and has rendered its "yes" to God concerning all
> of this, since now God's will and the soul's are one through
> their own free consent, then the soul has attained the posses-
> sion of God insofar as this is possible by the way of will and
> grace. And this means that in the "yes" of the soul, God has
> given the true and complete "yes" of his grace. This is a high
> state of spiritual espousal between the soul and the Word, in
> which the Bridegroom favors it and frequently pays it loving
> visits by which it receives intense delight.[15]

The characteristics of spiritual marriage

In his classic work, *The Theology of Christian Perfection*, Fr. Royo Marín attributes three qualities to spiritual marriage:

1. *Transformation into the Beloved:* the soul is penetrated by God's grace to such an extent that, although the faculties of the souls remain intact, they become completely docile to their corresponding theological virtues: intellect/faith, memory/hope, will/love, thus rendering the soul divine by participation.

2. *Mutual surrender:* the inevitable consequence of transformation of the soul into God, in which the two spouses give totally of each to each other. St. Paul refers to this when he reminds the Corinthians that he married them to Christ (2 Cor. 11:2). Nonetheless, full awareness of this married state is given to the few.

3. *Permanent union in love:* to these souls is given not only the awareness of their married state, but the almost habitual awareness of the presence of the Blessed Trinity in their souls, by way of visions and other extraordinary phenomena.[16]

Although most of the mystical writers who have treated the theme of spiritual marriage have been women, the vocation is universal. Linguistically it may cause some difficulties in English when male saints speak in these terms. Whereas the female saints use no qualifiers, those male mystical writers (St. John of the Cross and St. Pio of Pietralcina, for example) who have written of their own matrimonial relationship with

God speak of him as "the Spouse of my soul," benefiting from
the almost universal feminine noun for soul: *alma* (Sp.), *anima*
(It.), *Seele* (Ger.), *âme* (Fr.), etc.

Wedding Day

The day of St. Thérèse's espousals with Christ, she carried a
letter to him on her heart:

September 8, 1890

O Jesus, my Divine Spouse! May I never lose the second robe
of my baptism! Take me before I can commit the slightest vol-
untary fault. May I never seek nor find anything but yourself
alone. May creatures be nothing for me and may I be nothing
for them, but may You, Jesus, be *everything!* May the things
of earth never be able to trouble my soul, and may nothing
disturb my peace. Jesus, I ask You for nothing but peace, and
also love, Infinite love without any limits other than yourself;
love which is no longer I but You, my Jesus. Jesus, may I die
a martyr for You. Give me the martyrdom of heart or body,
or rather give me both. Give me the grace to fulfil my Vows
in all their perfection, and make me understand what a real
spouse of yours should be. Never let me be a burden to the
community, let nobody be occupied with me, let me be looked
upon as one to be trampled underfoot, forgotten like Your little grain of sand, Jesus. May your will be done in me perfectly,
and may I arrive at the place You have prepared for me.

Jesus, allow me to save very many souls; let no soul be
lost today; let all the souls in purgatory be saved. Jesus, pardon me if I say anything I should not say. I want only to give
You joy and to console You.[17]

Manuscript B, written exactly six years later, reveals that this prayer was heard and fully lived out. Only divine and eternal Love, God himself, who embraces all times and places, all persons and vocations entrusted to them and is "everything" to Thérèse, gives Thérèse, too, the possibility to be "everything," without falling into pantheism:

> Yes, I have found my place in the Church and it is You, O my God, who have given me this place; in the heart of the Church, my Mother, I shall be *Love*. Thus I shall be everything, and thus my dream will be realized.[18]

Being love, for Thérèse, was an all-encompassing vocation which gradually extended itself in the four directions open to love: spousal, maternal, filial, and ultimately, fraternal.

Spousal love

Upon professing her vows and binding herself canonically to Christ, she could call Christ her Spouse for the first time.[19] Indeed, her writings refer to her nuptial relationship with Christ citing *Song of Songs* 47 times. But rather than an intimist or myopic spirituality, we discover a zealous heart that knew how to turn this relationship with Christ to apostolic advantage, using its privileged position to intercede for souls. Thérèse's entire theology can be summarized as "loving Christ and making Christ loved."[20] Incarnating the love of Christ pulls Thérèse's heart in four directions: spousal, maternal, filial, and fraternal. This should cause no surprise since Christ himself calls himself spouse (Mt. 9:15; 22:2; 26:1–13; Lk. 12:36; Eph. 5:31–32; Rev. 19:7–10; 21:3), brother, and son to anyone who does the will of his father and possesses divine charity (Mk. 3:31–35). But as a consecrated soul, Thérèse's heart is first and foremost that of a spouse and of a mother. *"To be Your Spouse, to be a Carmelite, and by my union with You to be a Mother of souls, should not this suffice me?"*[21] Her writings contain rich teachings on Christian virginity, the fertile virginity that is inseparable from the Christ-centered marriage and maternity love, which allows her to participate in the life of her Beloved who says "she it was I loved and searched for from my youth; I resolved to have her as my bride" (Wis. 8:2). This spousal love is fire and passion in the pure heart, cleansed by the action and presence of the Holy Spirit, and fruit of a covenant relationship with God. This exclusive love for Jesus Christ permits her to exercise a universal love without sharing her heart.

Maternal love

Her maternal love springs from the heart of a mother who wants the best for her children, precisely what she has found: Christ and his salvation. She models her maternal love on the Blessed Virgin Mary, seeking to imitate her maternal qualities of hope, self-giving, and entrusting herself to divine Providence.[22] This spousal and maternal love permits her to trust unfailingly in the infinite mercy of her Beloved, since it is precisely this love which permits her to know the interior of her Beloved's Heart. She refers to her indivisibility of heart in not seeking human affection or affirmation from the nuns under her charge.

Filial love

She presents her filial love in the form of "the little way," this often misconstrued way of spiritual infancy which consists of complete trust in God. At the same time, the notion of spiritual infancy is protected from becoming infantile through its expression of loving fulfilment of the will of God and apostolic charity. Although this way produces spiritual children, it is certainly not for the spiritually infantile. Rather, it is fruit of theological virtue. This trust is authentic inasmuch as it is obedient. It requires a total dependence on God which never denies him the smallest detail. It is simply the Gospel: "If you love me, you will keep my commandments. And my Father and I will come to you and make our dwelling within you." (Jn. 14:23). "I understand and I know from experience," she says, "that *the Kingdom of God is within you*."[23] Such a program requires divine assistance in profound union with all one's heart, mind, and strength (Mt. 23:38). The dynamic of this little way is such that the more Thérèse becomes a child, the more she perfects her spousal and maternal love.

Thérèse's fraternal love would be extracted from her later in unexpected circumstances.

Love and darkness

Taking Fr. Marín's paradigm of spiritual marriage, it seems clear that Thérèse experienced the first two characteristics of spiritual marriage. Nonetheless, until the moment of her death, Thérèse never had visions nor did she want them, since her little way had more to do with the darkness of faith and the abandonment of trust than with extraordinary phenomena.[24] Her way was to be something imitable by all, just as spiritual marriage is a universal vocation.

But for those who arrive at the experiential level of spiritual marriage, namely the mystics, they find it always includes participation in his Christ's Passion. Again we find the dual fruit of espousals and participatory death, sprung from the seed of baptism, as referred to earlier in *Romans* 6:3–6. In Thérèse's case, her universal vocation (spouse) and its exterior form (Carmelite) were undeniable and flourishing. Nonetheless, she still lacked total lucidity with regard to her particular and unrepeatable mission.

> "To be Your Spouse, to be a Carmelite, and by my union with You to be a Mother of souls, should not this suffice me? And yet it is not so. No doubt, these three privileges sum up my true vocation: Carmelite, Spouse, Mother, and yet I feel within me other vocations. I feel the vocation of a WARRIOR, THE PRIEST, THE APOSTLE, THE DOCTOR, THE MARTYR. Finally, I feel the need and the desire of carrying out the most heroic of deeds for You, O Jesus. I feel within my soul the courage of the Crusader, the Papal Guard, and I would want to die on the field of battle in defense of the Church."[25]

Like St. Francis of Assisi, she too desired martyrdom, but unlike "the most saintly Italian and most Italian of saints," Thérèse's stigmata would be interior. These were not the musings of a fervent, naïve girl, rather, this burning desire was fruit of a mature love. But living in a French cloister does make martyrdom at the hands of Saracens unlikely. How does one satisfy such an urge and remain faithful to the true vocation? Once again she was cast into frustration and turmoil.

My vocation is love

Thinking to find an answer in the Scriptures during her morning meditation, she opened to chapter 12 of the *First*

Letter to the Corinthians. There she understood that the Church is made up of many different members with particular vocations. Although she was on to something, she had not quite found peace of soul. Then she came upon it:

> "'Yet strive after THE BETTER GIFTS, and I point out to you a yet more excellent way' and the Apostle explains how all the most PERFECT gifts are nothing without LOVE. That charity is the EXCELLENT WAY that leads most surely to God . . . Then in the excess of my delirious joy, I cried out: O Jesus, my Love . . . my vocation, at last I have found it . . . MY VOCATION IS LOVE."[26]

Finally, her soul could rest at ease. She knew God's will after all and had been living it already. Her ardent desire to have all of the aforementioned vocations was satisfied in the all-embracing and universal vocation to theological charity.

In other words, her maternal love was not exhausted in the salvation of Pranzini, but constituted her permanent mission. Suffering with and like her divine Spouse, she would fulfil her mission as a mother to lost souls, by incarnating love. Peace returned to her soul but the magnanimity of her mission perplexed her. It seemed folly to desire, in all her littleness, such an exalted and costly mission of victimhood. But once again, she had to have recourse to her faith: "As long as You desire it O my Beloved . . . "[27] The price of fidelity would be extracted from this young nun in an arduous, drawn out way until her last moment in this life. For Thérèse, being a bride of Christ could not be lived in any other way than as victim. Her vocation and mission were indivisible, just as the four dimensions of her love became inseparable. Therese's full identification with her crucified Spouse was brought about by her fraternal love for souls in danger of eternal loss. This brought her to take upon herself their own darkness. Nonetheless, the vast difference between Therese's darkness and theirs was that hers was a vicarious darkness of faith while theirs was a darkness brought on through a culpable loss of faith."[28] This process went into motion shortly after pronouncing her first vows as her first doubts about the reality of heaven began to torment her.[29] Her long Gethsemane had just begun.

In the shadow of the Cross

Thérèse would form part of that band of spiritual warriors with whom Christ shares his love in the two-fold fashion of espousals and redemptive suffering. From the moment of her self-oblation, Thérèse would experience "the oceans of graces that inundated her soul . . . the merciful love [which] renews and purifies her."[30] Nonetheless, her faith would be put to the test in ways she never expected or could have ever imagined. In fact, her trials and temptations against faith were so severe that those pertinent pages were originally suppressed so as not to cause scandal and confusion amongst the faithful.[31] Faced with such a trial of faith, it was Thérèse's marital fidelity that brought her living of espousal and victimhood with Christ to perfection. For Thérèse, any act or thought committed outside of God's will would constitute something akin to spiritual adultery or Pelagianism, thus severing the matrimonial bond.

If I were unfaithful, if I committed only the slightest infidelity, I feel that I would pay for it with frightful troubles, and I would no longer be able to accept death . . . for this (infidelity) would be relying upon my own strength, and when we do this, we run the risk of falling into the abyss.[32]

Thérèse shows a keen insight into the nature of sin by seeing it through the prism of union with Christ. If man was already created in God's image, then to develop this relationship with God through grace is to cooperate in the work of bringing this similarity to completion in the Person of Christ (cf. Col 1:15–20). Hence, to act against this covenant is not simply to step outside of a relationship, it is to destroy it even as one destroy one's similarity to Christ and the eternal plan over one's soul. Here we are confronted with the scandal of evil.

PART III

The Scandal of Evil

It is for judgement that I have come into the world, so that those without sight may see and those with sight turn blind.

—*Jn. 9:39*

Chapter 7

God's Unrequited Love

The real scandal of evil is born of pride in the form of disobedience. In a certain sense we can call every sin a declaration of independence from God, a *non serviam* (cf. Jer. 2:20). As an "offence against reason, truth and right conscience"[1] it places us in opposition to God, turning our hearts from him.

> Like the first sin, it is disobedience, a revolt against God through the will to become "like gods" [Gen. 3:5], knowing and determining good and evil. Sin is thus "love of oneself even to contempt of God." [*De civ. Dei.* 14,28] In this proud self-exaltation, sin is diametrically opposed to the obedience of Jesus, which achieves our salvation.[2]

Particularly exposed to temptations against faith are the learned and great, so says St. Thomas Aquinas. He states that the philosopher especially finds it hard to believe, since having attained a certain age of consciousness, he does not exempt himself from thinking through the opposing arguments raised by other philosophers or heretics. He attributes a certain heroism to such a confessor who, in refusing to abandon the truth of faith in spite of the arguments of violence, remains faithful. He can be compared to a martyr. The very fact that what he holds cannot be proven constitutes his predicament. All the man of faith can do is defend his own faith, since he cannot prove it or take the offensive.[3] Thérèse's "scandalous" faith difficulties would be of another nature: inculpable but nonetheless an occasion of spiritual danger if not dealt with prudently and valiantly.

Given the aforementioned nature of the act of faith's inseparability of "believing what God says is true, believing that he is God, and to committing oneself to God in faith," it can be asserted that sin is material, if not formal, atheism. For one cannot parse the denial of God's authority from the denial of his nature. Breaking out from the light of faith and charity, the soul is deprived of God's grace and presence. The soul has freely, albeit abusively, alienated itself from God, setting itself in a type of willed darkness.

The doctrine of atonement, justice, and justification

All of salvation history is a moving story of God's offering of love to his bride. His unrequited and unremitting love proves its mettle from original fall to our day. God's love has repeatedly condescended in mercy and re-established the covenant relationship with his chosen people. This covenant was definitively sealed on the cross as the Son of God gave birth to his bride, the Church, from his wounded side (Jn. 19:34). Such is

Christ's faithful, matrimonial love for his bride that all other marital love is simply a reflection of it and, as a sacrament, points to this greater reality. The spousal love of Christ for each soul is the reality (Eph. 5:25–27), any other type of love is a degree of allusion to it, for "God is love and he who remains in love remains in God and God in him" (1 Jn. 4:16).

Man's estrangement from God as a result of original sin could only by atoned for by God's intervention. While he could have done this directly through an act of the divine will, he chose to bring about redemption through full participation in man's lot.

> As He hung upon the Cross, Christ Jesus not only appeased the justice of the Eternal Father which had been violated, but He also won for us, His brethren, an ineffable flow of graces. it was possible for Him of Himself to impart these graces to mankind directly; but He willed to do so only through a visible Church made up of men, so that through her all might cooperate with Him in dispensing the graces of Redemption. As the Word of God willed to make use of our nature, when in excruciating agony He would redeem mankind, so in the same way throughout the centuries He makes use of the Church that the work begun might endure.[4]

The same Mystical Body that is the Church, although redeemed and rejoined to Christ, continues to suffer in its members. God's plan has willed it that, as members of the same Mystical Body, linked together as it were, one's suffering becomes another member's suffering. Further, as all the members share this pain, so too can the healthy members come to the assistance of the ailing. "So in the Church the individual members do not live for themselves alone, but also help their fellows, and all work in mutual collaboration for the common comfort and for the more perfect building up of the whole Body."[5]

> To me He has granted His *infinite Mercy* and *through it* I contemplate and adore other divine perfections! All of these perfections appear to be resplendent *with love*, even his Justice (and perhaps this even more so than the others) seems to be clothed in *love*.[6]

Seeing everything through the prism of mercy

Here we find another key with which to understand St. Thérèse's soul and theology. A saint recognizes a dominant attribute of the one, simple God and that attribute acts as a sort of prism through which he arrives at all the other attributes. Thérèse's experience of God's mercy permitted her to understand his divine Essence and his other attributes in a completely harmonious way with the Fathers of the Church as well as the Scholastic theologians and the Spanish mystical theologians. Pseudo-Dionysius approached God through the prism of his Goodness; for St. Anselm it was Justice; St. Thomas Aquinas saw him expressed through Being; and what St. John of the Cross knew theologically—that God was a fire within—he experienced mystically. St. Thérèse's is a narrative theology of Mercy, fruit of her experience and means for her apostolate. In it she reflects Paul's doctrine of justification as laid out in Romans 3:21–26. The formal cause of Divine Justice (*dikaiosúne*) is not judgement (*krínein*) of the sinner, but gratuitous justification (*dikaioun*) through the Blood of Christ.

Perhaps Thérèse's cure after long suffering under scruples acted as a protection against such caricatures common to her epoch. Her theology presents God as essentially merciful. Naturally, God is just and exercises just judgements. But in Thérèse's theology, just as St. Catherine of Siena intuited, there is a primacy of mercy. Hence her theology becomes a theology of hope in Divine Mercy.

Just as she had interceded for Pranzini after having received her Christmas grace, she would intercede for the salvation of all men on here Profession's Day: "Jesus, let me save many souls: don't let one of them be damned today."[7] Later, she would formulate her little way of confidence and love, and with the same confidence she would intercede for all atheists.

And this will was for us to be made holy by the offering
of his body made once and for all in Jesus Christ
—Heb. 10:10

Chapter 8

Vicarious Victimhood

A Deeper Participation in the Life
of the Divine Spouse

The pattern to follow

Thérèse of Lisieux lived her agony in communion with the
agony of Jesus, "experiencing" in herself the very paradox of
Jesus's own bliss and anguish: "In the Garden of Olives our
Lord was blessed with all the joys of the Trinity, yet his dying
was no less harsh. It is a mystery, but I assure you that, on
the basis of what I myself am feeling, I can understand something of it."[1]

The ultimate sacrificial victim is Jesus Christ: "*Here I am! I
am coming to obey your will . . .* and this *will* was for us to be
made holy by the *offering* of his *body* made once and for all
by Jesus Christ" (Heb. 10:9–10). As priest and victim (cf. Heb.
5:8–9) he made all other sacrifices useless. The motive for a
sacrificial victim in the biblical perspective is grounded in the
reality of the relationship between sin and its corresponding
redemption. Natural law requires such payment[2] as did the
revealed Law; but the price of man's redemption demanded

61

a divine victim. We sinners can merely invoke the merits of that sacrifice.

Having entered into a theological existence and advancing along the path of interior life, a person is confronted ever more profoundly with the reality of the effects of original sin in his soul. That the call to communion with God is fulfilled by means of the redemptive death of Christ should not reduce Christ's death to an instrumental cause or a historical fact. The very nature of the theological life transformed into spiritual marriage requires a full participation in the life of Christ. As Christ's life and death take over the life of the individual soul, so too everything the spouse of Christ thinks, speaks, and does becomes an prolongation of Christ's life and death: "I am suffering now, and in my own body to do what I can to make up all that still is to be undergone by Christ for the sake of his body, the Church" (Col. 1:26). Paul is proof that Christ's passion is lived out in an extraordinary way in extraordinary saints.

Victim-spouse

The concept of victim-spouses is not new to Christian thought. St. Ambrose treats of it at length and in great detail in his work *Concerning Virginity*.[3] The living tradition of the Church has always taken victim-spouses into particular consideration with Christ as the proto-victim-spouse for his Mystical Body the Church. The cross and death he bore have become the epicentre of all human suffering in which he still suffers in his members and his members in him. Given the nature of divine charity, which cannot love God without loving neighbour, the solidarity and communion of the victim with Christ drives that person to seek and relish those sufferings which will effect the salvation of other members of the Mystical Body. Although the concept of victim-spouse has been somewhat lost in modern theology, the phenomenon constantly renews itself in the "lived theology of the saints." Mystics participate in the *kodesh* (the utter sacredness) of God which, by nature, separates them from the profane, yet they are not separated from goings on of the world around them. Usually it is precisely the concrete and immediate human tragedies which provoke their heroic actions: "The only cause of my death is my zeal for the Church of God who devours and knows me. Accept, Lord, the sacrifice of my life for the Mystical Body of your holy Church!"[4] At the age of four years St. Catherine of Siena promised herself to Christ and was subsequently invited into spiritual marriage and victim-hood. And in more recent times, St. Gemma Galgani as well as St. Thérèse of Lisieux's contemporary Carmelite sister, Bl. Elizabeth of the Holy Trinity, were also accepted by God as victims. Such generous spouses are the occasion by which Christ renews his redemptive mystery in its entirety. The common denominators of this sacrifice are the heroic self offering of the spouse and God's acceptance of the gift of self. God's acceptance makes itself known materially through their martyring physical and spiritual suffering and, sometimes, accompanied through locutions or visions, such as was the case with St. Joan of Arc, St. Faustina Kowalska, and St. Pio of Pietrelcina.

Moving towards communion introduces the person to new depths of participation in the suffering and death of Christ. In the Blood of Christ expiation is accomplished (cf. Rom. 3:25) and sin is eliminated (Heb. 9:14) in the exchange of love, divine for human. Thus the bride is made ready for the marriage of the sacrificed Lamb (cf. Rev. 19:8) through incorporation into his expiatory mission.

It is only by the strength of extraordinary grace that these true spouses of Christ can bear the suffering heaped upon them[5]—often only ending at the moment of death, when at the height of spiritual perfection, these elected souls most resemble Christ Crucified. Victim souls are aware of the efficacy of their sacrifice and willing consent in the name of the countless souls they save from perdition. Their physical and moral sorrow becomes the cause of their joy and inseparable communion with Christ in this life as well as the assurance of the crown of victory in heaven.

Father and victim

Thérèse did not have to look far for living examples of our Lord's victim souls. She may very well have been inspired by her father's own generous self-offering. She relates how her father (at the time of this writing a servant of God) already known for never having uttered a word of criticism against another person, suffered as God, one by one, took his daughters from him leaving him a lone widower. During a visit to his daughters' convent, however, he exclaimed "My God, it is too much! Yes, I'm too happy. I'll never make it to Heaven this way. I want to suffer something for you. I offer myself . . . " The saint mentions how he stopped himself not daring to utter the word "victim," but as she says " . . . we had understood."[6]

Worldly minds might find such sentiments perplexing. Human nature rebels against suffering and there is nothing natural about desiring it. But as we have seen, the theological life is beyond nature, it is supernatural. The life of union brings the follower of Christ to be transformed into him and makes of suffering a fruitful penitence and a holocaust of oneself. It is the final proof of the purity of intention behind the declaration of love for Christ, a love which must be proved if it is to grow.

*I appeal to you therefore, brethren, by the mercies of
God, to present your bodies as a living sacrifice, holy
and acceptable to God, which is your spiritual worship.*

—Rom. 12:1

Chapter 9

Thérèse's Act of Oblation to Merciful Love

Love desires to suffer with the Beloved

Pope John Paul II began the new millennium by inviting the
entire Church to discover Christ through personal sanctity.
He proposed Thérèse of Lisieux as an example of a saint who
fathomed the depths of union with Christ and discovered that
experiencing Christ in this life brings with it the dual experience of love and suffering:

> The saints offer us precious insights which enable us to
> understand more easily the intuition of faith, thanks to the
> special enlightenment which some of them have received
> from the Holy Spirit, or even through their personal experience of those terrible states of trial which the mystical tradition describes as the "dark night." Not infrequently the saints
> have undergone *something akin to Jesus' experience on the Cross*
> in the paradoxical blending of bliss and pain. *Thérèse of Lisieux*
> lived her agony in communion with the agony of Jesus, "experiencing" in herself the very paradox of Jesus's own bliss and

anguish: "In the Garden of Olives our Lord was blessed with all the joys of the Trinity, yet his dying was no less harsh. It is a mystery, but I assure you that, on the basis of what I myself am feeling, I can understand something of it."[1]

The Holy Father compares St. Thérèse's suffering to the vicarious suffering of Christ in Gethsemane. The mission of suffering in order to save atheists was something Thérèse sought and God granted it to her. "Never would I have believed it was possible to suffer so much! Never! Never! I cannot explain this except by the ardent desire I have to save souls."[2]

To understand the particular mission St. Thérèse received, the spiritual and cultural context of late Nineteenth Century France has to be kept in mind. This was the time of the construction of Montmartre, the place of perpetual Eucharistic adoration in reparation to the Sacred Heart of Jesus. Devotion to the Sacred Heart was at its height and maintained there in great part by French and Spanish preachers and spiritual writers. Congregations devoted to the Sacred Heart flourished and the French Carmelite convents added a canon to their constitutions permitting their members to offer themselves as vicarious victim souls in order to win graces for otherwise lost souls. Manuscript B is reminiscent of Sacred Heart/atonement vocabulary. It stresses Christ's sacred Humanity and uses St. Margaret Mary's description of Christ who seeks love and finds so little. Thérèse reveals that her desire for martyrdom and for all vocations could only be realized and summarized by love,[3] and the "smallest act of pure love is more valuable than all works together."[4] "One day I hope that You, the Adorable Eagle, will come to fetch me, your little bird; and ascending with it to the Furnace of Love, You will plunge it for all eternity into the burning Abyss of the Love to which it has offered itself as victim."[5]

The historical context of Thérèse's Act of Oblation

Considering Europe's spiritual state, Thérèse and her sisters had ample motivation to offer themselves. The anticlericalism raging in Thérèse's France was merely one expression of an atheistic ideology and a well thought out program to change the face of humanity. Cardinal de Lubac's work *The Drama of Atheistic Humanism* finds the roots for the Twentieth Century's gulags and concentration camps in the Western Europe of the mid to late Nineteenth Century. He says "It is not true, as is sometimes said, that man cannot organize the world without God. What is true is that, without God, he can only organize it against man."[6] Thérèse was well aware of the spiritual battle sweeping across her country; she had an atheist and anticlerical relative by marriage who worked for a government increasingly antagonistic to the Church. This was the time when new scientific discoveries and mere theories thought to discredit the Church. This was the milieu in which Thérèse grew up and would struggle in her faith.

Central to our study is a particular grace St. Thérèse received from our Lord on the Feast of the Holy Trinity, June 9th, 1895, and St. Thérèse's cooperation with it. Lost in thoughts about the example of certain mystics who had offered themselves to Christ as victim-souls generously taking upon themselves the just punishments of other sinners, Thérèse asked herself if she could do the same. She hesitated at the prospect. Her inadequacy was no match for such a task.

Nonetheless, she refused to interrupt this interior movement of the Holy Spirit, finally breaking into spontaneous prayer:

"O my God! Will your Justice alone find souls willing to immolate themselves as victims? Does not Your Merciful Love need them too? On every side this love is unknown, rejected; those hearts upon whom You would lavish it turn to creatures, seeking happiness from them with their miserable affection; they do this instead of throwing themselves into Your arms and of accepting Your infinite Love. O my God! Is Your disdained Love going to remain closed up within Your Heart? It seems to me that if You were to find souls offering themselves as victims of holocaust to Your Love, You would consume them rapidly; it seems to me, too, that You would be happy not to hold back the waves of infinite tenderness within You. If Your Justice loves to release itself, this Justice which extends only over the earth, how much more does Your Merciful Love desire to set souls on fire since Your Mercy reaches to the heavens. O my Jesus, let me be this happy victim; consume Your holocaust with the fire of Your Divine Love."[7]

The flames of divine love which punish the unrepentant and purge the impure would turn on her. As a pure soul, she experienced the fire as the pain of love.[8] In fact, she relates that the flames penetrated her soul to such an extent that she lost any trepidation before the very prospect of purgatory, of which she had previously considered herself unworthy. This newest experience of God proved St. John's words true: "fear is driven out by perfect love" (I Jn. 4:18). Any worry about littleness or inadequacy that she might have had was abandoned as she abandoned herself to the hands of God. With her superior's blessing she made a formal "Act of Oblation to Merciful Love: offering my self as a victim of Holocaust to God's Merciful Love." In her two page long consecration as victim, Thérèse reveals the depths of her love and the consequences of its four dimensions.

The nature of her oblation

The text of the Act of Oblation has three goals:

1. *Union:* "I desire to accomplish Your will perfectly and to reach the degree of glory You have prepared for me ... Since You have loved me so much as to give me your only Son as my Saviour and my Spouse, the infinite treasures of His merits are mine ... I ask you to come take possession of my soul. ... I do not want to lay up merits for heaven. I want to work for your love alone with one purpose of pleasing You, consoling your Sacred Heart, and of saving souls who will love You eternally."

2. *Atonement:* "I want to console You for the ingratitude of the wicked ... "

3. *Apostolate:* "I desire to Love You and make You Loved, to work for the glory of Holy Church by saving souls on earth and liberating those suffering in purgatory ... "[9]

Here it is important to underline several characteristics of this self-offering. First of all, its birth was occasioned by seemingly random thoughts. From these thoughts, she came to the firm conviction of God's particular mission for her, and received her superior's blessing. Thereupon, she then made her formal Act of Oblation. In other words, we witness here a display of how God's providence respects yet uses human liberty to complete his eternal plan, all bound together by obedience and love. The Holy Spirit used what were her own thoughts to inspire in her the Father's will. St. Thérèse explains how the fire of God's Love, the Holy Spirit "draws her" or attracts her so as to make her run together with Him,[10] thus living as a sojourner during her earthly life until she reaches the state of fullness of realization her entire being in Heaven. As faithful spouse of Christ, Thérèse cannot but desire what Christ desires.

Second, her self-offering becomes the particular mission which divine Providence intended for a particular time and place. Thus her nuptials with Christ is inseparable from her apostolate, and in being drawn to God, she in turn, brings her entrusted souls in her wake: "When a soul allows herself to be captivated by the odor of your ointments, she cannot run alone, all the souls whom she loves follow in her train."[11] In a certain sense, souls become her dowry. Christ not only receives her but all her treasures as well. She counts her entrusted souls amongst her dearest treasures and trusts unhesitatingly that Christ will accept them along with her own gift of self.[12]

Third, as she initially surmised, such a mission certainly was beyond her own possibilities. But her strength is found elsewhere—in him who gives power to her weakness (Rm. 5:20),[13] for "the weaker the soul, the more efficacious is the love if disposed to be a victim."[14] Further, given that her mission is God's initiative, Thérèse felt complete confidence: "suffering of my own doing I could never bear, but those permitted me by God's will" are accompanied by his grace to bear them.[15]

Becoming one spirit with God

Human, matrimonial love produces union of purpose, it brings about growth in mutual love and new life. The bond wrought by theological love brings about a mutual penetration of the two beings it unites, thus bringing about transformation of the lesser into the greater by participation. Cooperation with charity under the influence of the Holy Spirit purifies the consecrated soul and permits this theological virtue to exercise with freedom of movement and the efficacy God desires for the soul.

The nature of Thérèse's spousal union with Christ drives her to embrace everything that he had to endure in his earthly life. Between the Christmas grace of Bethlehem and the interior trial of faith at Gethsemane, Thérèse continued to advance along the path of spousal, maternal and filial love. And as she advanced, the fourth dimension of her love emerged. She became sister to the impious.[16]

Fraternal love

Her fraternal love is revealed in its fullness only in the last years of her brief life, primarily in. *Manuscript C* (11v–31r). Here she offers an extensive account of her experience of fraternal charity. Love cannot remain static. Thérèse's love for Christ identified her with her Beloved to the point of making her sister to "all men."

John Paul II writes:

"This interior maturity and spiritual greatness in suffering are certainly the result of a particular conversion and cooperation with the grace of the crucified Redeemer. It is He

Himself who acts at the heart of human sufferings through His Spirit of truth, through the consoling Spirit. It is He who transforms, in a certain sense, the very substance of the spiritual life, indicating for the person who suffers a place close to Himself."[17]

If suffering brings about conversion and a particular solidarity among sufferers,[18] then suffering desired and accepted out of love for Christ and souls brings about communion with him. But an eminently apostolic practical person such as St. Thérèse of Lisieux saw such suffering as an opportunity to win that same conversion and solidarity for souls in the darkness of disbelief.

> "I desire to love You and make You loved, . . . by saving souls on earth. Since You loved me so much as to give me Your only Son as my Savior and my Spouse, the infinite treasures of His merits are mine. I offer them to You with gladness, . . . I thank you, o my God! for all the graces You have granted me, especially the grace of making me pass through the crucible of suffering . . . in order to live in one single act of perfect love, I OFFER MYSELF AS A VICTIM OF HOLOCAUST TO YOUR MERCIFUL LOVE."[19]

Indeed, such generous self-giving is proof of faith, hope, and charity refined to perfection. With St. Paul Thérèse can say "I have been crucified with Christ; it is no longer I who live, but Christ who lives in me: and the life I now live in the flesh I live by faith in the Son of God, who loved me and gave himself for me" (Gal. 2:19–20). For this is not simply fruit of lived experience but a case of grace perfecting a soul. The same *scientia amoris* which led Christ to the Cross extends an open invitation to accompany him there. If he expressed his love chiefly through his suffering and death, it is then in this way that he lives in the interior of those who love him to the point of transforming union.

If it was faithful love that opened Thérèse up to the suffering of her Beloved and invited her to take it upon herself, paradoxically, it was this same purifying love which made her feel abandoned by the one she loved. This was a further participation in Christ's Golgotha abandonment.

PART IV

Dark Nights of Atheism and of Faith

Blessed are the pure of heart for they shall see God.

—Mt. 5:8

Chapter 10

The Will to Believe and the Will to Power

If certain souls have chosen actions resulting in darkness and alienation from God, still other souls have taken such symptoms of alienation upon themselves as a fuller, more intimate yet paradoxical share in Christ's life. The history of the Church presents us with spiritual theologians and mystics who describe varying accounts of such darkness, each one with a host of different implications and manifestations according to his own particular circumstances, needs, and character, or simply God's inscrutable designs. "It is an ancient doctrine, emphasized by apophatic theologians and mystics, that God dwells in inaccessible light, a light so searingly absolute that it cancels out all images and ideas we may form of him, veiling the divine glory"[1] in a "dark night of nothingness" or "fog"[2] as St. Thérèse of Lisieux described her experience.[3] Pseudo-Dionysius[4] was the first to report such phenomenon. William of Thierry,[5] St. Jane Frances de Chantal,[6] St. Paul of the Cross,[7] St. John of the Cross,[8] St. Pio of Pietrelcina,[9] and Bl. Teresa of

Calcutta[10] have all suffered and described their own trials of darkness of faith. William of Thierry claims to have found joy in his darkness, trusting that charity would make up for what lacked in his intellect. The fickle winds of sentiment and feeling prove themselves an unworthy foundation for a serious interior life for they are too easily let down or seduced. Therefore, the way of the theological virtues, above all charity, is the only sure path, for nothing short of them will stand up to satanic assaults on the soul during such a trial.[11]

Thérèse repeatedly heard a mocking voice

"You are dreaming about the light, about a fatherland embalmed in the sweetest of perfumes; you are dreaming about the *eternal* possession of the Creator of all the marvels; you believe that one day you will walk out of this fog which surrounds you! Advance, advance, advance; rejoice in death which will give you not what you hope for but a night still more profound, the night of nothingness."[12]

The oppressions of her childhood returned to keep vigil by her deathbed:

When I arose early this morning (August 6th, 1897), I found my dear little sister pale and disfigured by suffering and anguish. She said: 'The devil is all around me; I don't see him but I feel him. He is tormenting me; he is holding me with an iron hand to prevent me from taking the slightest relief; he is increasing my pains in order to make me despair. And I can no longer pray! I can only look at the Blessed Virgin and say: "Jesus!" how necessary is that prayer at Compline:

procul recedant omnia et noctium phantasmata! Deliver us from the phantoms of the night.

"I experience something mysterious. Until now, I've suffered especially in my right side, but God asked me if I wanted to suffer for you, and I immediately answered that I did. At that same instant, my left side was seized with an incredible pain. *I'm suffering for you*, and the devil doesn't want it!"[13]

Shades of darkness

Whereas in earlier mystical writers the interior struggle is marked by worry and doubt with regard to one's relationship with God, St. Thérèse's experience is unique in its temptation to blaspheme while confronted with the specter of eternal nothing. Perhaps this should not surprise us. The Church's mystical tradition was developed in times that knew no formal atheism. But the spiritual children of the Enlightenment—of which the French Revolution's atrocities were only one manifestation—were educated to darkness. An age which has seen political systems built on atheistic dialectical materialism in the East and the consumerist version in the West needs such victims to suffer in expiation for its willed darkness. Certainly, God uses this as a means of purification of the saint's soul; but this interior circumstance, as any aspect of one's life, can be offered up for the salvation of those souls most in need. Indeed, some saints seem to be called to suffer precisely such darkness as a vicarious suffering to save those souls who have affirmed their own particular brand of atheism.

Alongside the systematic and institutional atheism for which St. Thérèse would suffer, a more subtle and therefore more insidious form arose as well. A contemporary of St. Thérèse's was Cardinal John Henry Newman who summed up the bourgeois and condescending general attitude of their age in the following terms:

> Men are inclined to wait quietly to see whether proofs of the actuality of revelation will drop into their laps, as though they were in the position of arbitrators and not in that of the needy. They have decided to test the Almighty in a passionless judicial fashion, with total lack of bias, with sober minds. It is a fatal error to approach the truth with anything less than homage."[14]

Either form is enough to lose God, therefore both require expiation.

The will to power: isolating self-love

Discussing the nature of the scandal of evil, we saw sin as a phenomenon of human life, a contradiction of one's own nature, a rebellion against God and others. But such is the depth of original sin's effects in the soul of man that, with time, entire systems of thought would be founded on his rebellion against God, elevating it to an ideal. In such disorder, love turns from the other and towards itself, thus becoming egoism.

Perhaps we should distinguish between healthy, natural love of self and egoism. Deep within each person there is a natural, spontaneous love of self, which, as all of God's work, is good. This underlies love of neighbour. But this initial love rarely retains its original purity. As soon as it springs up it is muddied by a self-directed glance, which almost inevitably engenders egoism. We might explain this by saying that the pristine "I," in an immediate and very hidden movement turns into a "me." This subtle twist is the beginning of isolation, the birth of pride.

The transition from "I" to "me," from a good, natural love of self to the disordered love of egoism, happens before we are aware of it. As a subtle and delicate shift, we are rarely aware of its taking place. The fetters it creates go so deep that we can scarcely break them without a real death to self.

This is the renunciation of self, the dying to self of which the Gospel speaks. Egoism, the most prevalent of all parasites, feeds on the spontaneous love that images God. In directing this love toward the "me" egoism empties love of all substance and corrupts it. Such was the desire to "become like gods" (cf. Gen 3:5) that tempted Adam and Eve. Such is the "will to power" of Friedrich Nietzsche.[15] The effects of original sin have the power to vitiate and twist the answers to any and all questions: "I love" becomes "I love myself"; "I seek happiness" becomes "I seek my happiness at any cost"; "I seek the truth" becomes "I create my own truth." The distinctions are subtle because egoism uses the terms of love and truth so as to give the appearance of legitimacy. The crowning effect of original sin, when we have surrendered ourselves to it, is to exalt oneself as the ultimate authority, thus deposing God in one's life, if only temporarily through an actual sin or permanently through a defining system of thought founded on such principles.[16]

Friedrich Nietzsche, a contemporary of St. Thérèse of Lisieux, rebelled against his strict religious upbringing. Following the lead of Auguste Comte[17] and the positivists, he held that man has no organ with which he can know God and, were he to exist, man is unequipped to attain God, thus making the God of Christianity irrelevant. Further, since Christians notoriously live as if they do not believe in God, Nietzsche can announce God's death and all its nihilistic consequences with impunity: nothing transcends man, no authority obliges him to obedience any longer. And this "nothing" that transcends man is precisely Nietzsche's point.

Man has grown up and left his childish religious ways and, in doing so, left God for dead. This new "adult" world is on its own in total autonomy capable of solving all its problems for itself. It lives in a sort of perpetual Holy Saturday,[18] having recently slain the divine One and not expecting to have news of him in the near future, we can get along without any thought about him. "God is dead and we have killed him."

Given this newly found absolute sovereignty of the human will, knowledge of God through faith, spiritual spontaneity, and love all become unworthy of a man who wants to truly live. Such was Nietzsche's influence that Western society claims his patrimony even today: the modern understanding of the will divorced from truth, unilateral relationships founded on utility, and virtually everything overshadowed by claims of absolute freedom, made available thanks to moral indifference. Having successfully separated love and truth from the will, Nietzsche's vision of relationship becomes characterized by command and obedience.[19]

Nonetheless, Nietzsche notes, there are still many subjugated to the God of Christianity. Therefore, everyone is left with two alternatives: Renunciation of freedom (liberty) and abandonment to God's servitude according to the Christian model; or the way of the *Übermensch* which accepts life by embracing it with all its limitless pleasures and claims the position of command in total freedom (libertinism).

The Way of Spiritual Childhood

In contrast to Nietzsche's childishness the way of spiritual childhood leads us to be supernaturally ourselves without the defects of natural childhood. Amongst the hallmarks of spiritual childhood simplicity is perhaps the most prominent. It confounds hypocrisy and is capable of grasping profound truths in an existential way, as opposed to intellectualist. The spiritual child understands the truth in terms of an immediate relationship to it without the filter of the theoretical or the ability of wishing it away.

The awareness of one's littleness engenders more confidence than fear. Indigence and weakness, conscious that, on our own, we are incapable of anything in the order of salvation or sanctification moves the soul to seek God's strength. Educated in this humility, the spiritual child's faith becomes more sure than the trust of any natural child in the best of fathers. Such a child knows that the arms of God reach down to it to lift it high, just as Thérèse described the divine elevator.

This trust equips the spiritual child for the trials that await him.

The spiritual child becomes an icon of seemingly contradictory qualities and virtues: meekness and fortitude, simplicity and prudence, love and righteous anger.

Another point of capital importance is that when well understood the way of spiritual childhood wonderfully harmonizes also true humility with the desire for the loving contemplation of the mysteries of salvation. Thereby we see that this contemplation, which proceeds from living faith illumined by the gifts of understanding and wisdom, is in the normal way of sanctity. This penetrating and at times sweet contemplation of the mysteries of faith is not something extraordinary like visions, revelations,, and the stigmata, extrinsic favors, so to speak, which we do not find in the life of St. Thérèse of Lisieux; it is, on the contrary, the normal fruit of sanctifying grace, called grace of the virtues and the gifts and the seed of glory. It is the normal prelude of eternal life. This point of doctrine stands out clearly in the writings of St. Thérèse of the Child Jesus.[20]

In her own words we see this expressed:

To remain little is to recognize one's nothingness, to expect everything from God, as a little child expects everything from his father; it is to be disturbed about nothing, not to earn a fortune.

Even amongst poor people. As long as the child is quite small, they give him what he needs; but as soon as he has grown up, his father no longer wishes to feed him what he needs and says to him, "Work now, you can be self-supporting." Well, so as to never hear that, I have not wished to grow up, since I feel myself incapable of earning my living, the eternal life of heaven. I have, therefore, always remained little, having no other occupation than to gather the flowers of love and sacrifice and to offer them to God for His pleasure.

To be little also means not to attribute to oneself the virtues that one practices, believing oneself capable of something; but it means recognizing that God places this treasure of virtue in the hand of His little child that he may make use of it when necessity arises; and it is always God's treasure.[21]

It makes me happy to suffer for you, as I am suffering
now, and in my own body to do what I can to make up
all that has still to be undergone by Christ for the sake
of his Body, the Church.

—Eph. 1:24

Chapter 11

Thérèse's Darkness: Atonement
Adequate to its Epoch

The will to believe and the communion of love

Nietzsche's nihilism has the last word because he says so.
Thérèse's faith has the last word because her certainty is
founded in Someone else. Her faith anchors her in God,[1] in
something not of her own making, entrusted to Someone who
protects her from the threatening abyss of nihilism. In reject-
ing his childhood faith, Nietzsche has set himself afloat on
a raft of his own making which denies anything beyond the
ocean surface. But his worldview is not impermeable and he
knows it, for he has only made his view, not the world. And
the question every man is bound to put to himself about God
and eternity, human limits, and all that lies beyond them, are
reflected in Nietzsche's assertion that all pleasure yearns for
eternity, yet experiences itself only as a moment. The incom-
pleteness of man left to himself prevents him from resting in
his own self-sufficiency. Finally, in his manic *Ecce Homo*, he

admits "God or a buffoon—that is what I cannot choose, that is what I am."[2]

Unlike Nietzsche, for Thérèse, God's hidden-ness had more to do with her own incapacity than a defect on God's part. Whereas the philosopher fought against the immensity of All, the theologian stood her ground against the whispers of Nothing. Both were compelled to make a leap of faith Nietzsche claims he was not willing to make. Thérèse's faith (*amén*) cast her into darkness and her understanding (*amén*) was threatened, but she held her ground (*amén*) because she had abandoned herself (*amén*) to One who did understand.

Awareness of each other keeps people like Thérèse and Nietzsche from closing in on themselves. But whereas Thérèse's heroism and warrior-like spirit invites emulation, there is something poignant in a lone man's life-long tirade against Someone who does not, at least for him, exist.

Bernanos said of Thérèse:

> the message this saint brings to the world is one of the most mysterious and impressive ever seen. The world is dying for lack of infancy and it is precisely against this that the totalitarian demigods point their canons and tanks.[3]

In the mystery of the Incarnation, the Son of God has taken up the littleness of humanity; and in the mystery of redemption, he humbled himself more still. Through Thérèse's spousal love for Christ, she inserted herself into these mysteries and made them her own. Thérèse's little way or spiritual infancy united her to the greatness of Divinity, where all darkness and suffering find Someone who understands. Whereas both World Wars found their roots in Nineteenth Century materialist ideology, multitudes of soldiers in trenches, prisoners in concentration camps, and civilians alike during both those wars found counsel and consolation in Thérèse's autobiography.

The Nature of Thérèse's trial

Christ redeemed suffering. And those to whom he had entrusted a particular mission within the Church receive a portion of his suffering according to the grandeur of their mission. As the soul advances along the way of intimacy with Christ it grows in resemblance to the Beloved.

The common opinion is that the servants of God are more particularly tried, whether it be that they need a more profound purification, or whether, following the example of our Lord, they must work by the same means as He used for a great spiritual cause, such as the foundation of a religious order or the salvation of many souls. St. John of the Cross and St. Teresa almost continually experienced this, as the facts clearly show.[4]

About this Pope John Paul II writes:

The saints offer us precious insights which enable us to understand more easily the intuition of faith, thanks to the special enlightenment which some of them have received from the Holy Spirit, or even through their personal experience of those terrible states of trial which the mystical tradition describes as the "dark night." Not infrequently the saints have undergone *something akin to Jesus' experience on the Cross* in the paradoxical blending of bliss and pain.[5]

The Holy Father is referring to the phenomenon undergone by mystics in which the soul's faculties experience a purification of such drastic proportions whose effects often leave the sufferer with temptations against faith, hope, and most particularly, against divine charity. Although this experience has been described by patristic authors such as St. Gregory of Nyssa in his *On the Song of Songs* and Pseudo-Dionysius' *Mystical Theology*, it was Thérèse's spiritual father who made a treatise of the subject in his *Dark Night of the Soul*. In it, St. John of the Cross gives a litmus test by which to judge the authenticity of a classical dark night experience: One finds no consolation in God or created things (see Thérèse's description of her habitual dryness in Ms C, 5v); although one's memory is fixed on God, one feels oneself to be slipping backwards (Thérèse underwent this trial, cf. *Epilogue*, p.266); in spite of constant effort, one finds it impossible to meditate (see Ms B, 1r; Ms C, 6v; Ms C, 7r). But more profoundly, the soul undergoing a dark night experience is tempted against faith in God; such are the symptoms. The reason for this suffering is purgation of one's own sins and attachments.[6]

Without subtracting from her suffering (she had most of the painful symptoms!), it seems that St. Thérèse's dark night experience does not fit St. John's definition in its strictest sense. She states clearly that hers was not a necessary purgation of attachments to sin.[7] In fact, as we have seen, upon making her general confession, her confessor Fr. Pichon solemnly declared that she had never committed a single mortal sin in her life.[8] Further, her case is not one of temptations against the existence of God, but of the existence of heaven:

Just as the genius of Christopher Columbus gave him the presentiment of a new world when nobody had even thought of such a thing; so also I felt that another land would one day serve me as a permanent dwelling place. Then suddenly the fog that surrounds me becomes more dense; it penetrates my soul and envelopes it in such a way that it is impossible to discover within it the sweet image of my Fatherland; everything has disappeared! When I want to rest my heart fatigued by the darkness that surrounds it by the memory of the luminous country after which I aspire, my torment redoubles.[9]

In other words, we are confronted with a different kind of darkness, a darkness of reparation and solidarity. Masters of the spiritual life have reported such a phenomenon, most notable, Fr. Reginald Garrigou-Lagrange.

When this trial is chiefly reparatory, when it has principally for its end to make the already purified soul work for the salvation of neighbour, then it preserves the same lofty characteristics (as the purificatory night of the spirit), but takes on an additional character more reminiscent of the intimate sufferings of Jesus and Mary, who did not need to be purified.[10]

Thérèse's darkness as solidarity

The dark night of the mystics offers us a greater insight into the intuition of faith, says the Holy Father. It also seems to give us a greater insight into the state of the world for which they intercede. In Thérèse's case she accepted her interior trial in fraternal love for her incredulous brothers.

I was unable to believe there were really impious people who had no faith. I believed they were actually speaking against their convictions when they denied the existence of heaven, that beautiful heaven where God Himself wanted to be their Eternal Reward. . . . Jesus made me feel that there really were souls who have no faith, and who, through the abuse of grace, lost this precious treasure, the source of the only real and pure joys. He permitted my soul to be invaded by thickest darkness, and that the thought of heaven, up until then so sweet to me, be no longer anything but the cause of struggle and torment. This trial was not a few days or a few weeks, it was not to be extinguished until the hour set by God Himself and this hour has not yet come. . . . One would have to travel through this dark tunnel to understand its darkness.[11]

Her trial reached to the core of her soul to such an extent that she identified herself with the atheists for whom she vicariously suffered.

Your child, however, O Lord, has understood Your divine light, and she begs pardon for her brothers. She is resigned to eat the bread of sorrow as long as You desire it; she does not wish to rise up from this table filled with bitterness at which poor sinners are eating until the day set by You. Can she not say in her name and in the name of her brothers, *"Have pity on us, O Lord, for we are poor sinners!"*[12]

She would not only have particular repercussions for her contemporaries, but for subsequent ages as well.

This youngest of all Doctors of the Church, St. Thérèse, is also the closest to us in time. There is a continuity which links all Doctors of the Church as a witness of the unchanging Gospel and, with the light and strength that come from the Holy Spirit, they become messengers, returning to proclaim it in its purity to their contemporaries."[13]

A saint is never distant from the world's plight. The drama of sin and grace taking place touches the saint directly. With a similar maternal instinct and a solid theological understanding of the nature of the Mystical Body of Christ similar to that of St. Catherine of Siena who constantly interceded for her souls as if she had committed their sins and asking our Lord pardon for her part in them,[14] so too does St. Thérèse of the Child Jesus immediately go about the business of seeking a solution and reparation for the sins of her contemporaries. In a world darkened by disbelief, the saint suffers trials of faith; in the order of grace, the saint acts as God's channel and beacon.

The mission of victim soul is fraught with dangers and temptations of every sort.

> In this case, the suffering makes one think of that of a lifesaver who, in a storm, struggles heroically to save from death those who are on the point of drowning. Spiritual lifesavers, like St. Paul of the Cross, struggle not only for hours or months, but sometimes for years in order to snatch souls from eternal death; and, in a way, these reparative souls must resist the temptations of the souls they seek to save that they may come efficaciously to their assistance.[15]

Thérèse's immediate reaction to her own trials of faith and the darkening gloom of atheism was to increase her acts of faith—to live an ever increasingly intense life of the theological virtues.

Thérèse as expiatory victim

The paradox of power in weakness is manifest throughout the life of Christ. This is his way. St. Thérèse fits into this logic perfectly. His seeming defeat in being crucified is also his victorious "being lifted up" (Jn. 3:13) which displays the triumph of human suffering over evil because it is infused with the salvific presence and will of God. "Yet if one suffers as a Christian, let him not be ashamed, but under that name let him glorify God" (1 Pet. 4:16).

As bride and as apostle, St. Thérèse participated in the suffering of the Mystical Body, in the suffering of the Head. Her expiation takes the form of their suffering, foremost, the trial of faith. In other words, rather than a condescending act of trying to help "that lot over there" she is initiated into their darkness of faith. In this Body, Christ wishes to be united with every individual and in a hidden way, he is united with those who suffer. With those who offer up their sufferings supernaturally, as an act of selfless love, he is united in a far more efficacious manner. For whoever willingly suffers in union with Christ—bears his tribulations in union with Christ—not only receives from Christ that strength already referred to but also "completes" by his suffering "what is lacking in Christ's suffering" (Col. 1:24). In other words, Christ, through his universal suffering, invites souls to participate in it—something

that can only be the fruit of the human free will in cooperation with God's grace and never imposed. That is what dis-
tinguishes the sought after pain of the masochist and the faith
filled relish of the soul in union with Christ.

> But how will I show my love, since love proves itself by
> deeds? . . . I wish to make profit out of the smallest actions
> and do them all for love. For Love's sake I wish to suffer
> and to rejoice: so shall I strew my flowers. Not one that I see
> but, singing all the while, I will scatter its petals before Thee.
> Should my roses be gathered from amid thorns, I will sing,
> notwithstanding, and the longer and sharper the thorns, the
> sweeter grow my song.[16]

Christ's Redemption is constantly taking place to differ-
ing degrees in assorted souls. Christ's participation in human
experience is not limited to the space/time limits of Jesus of
Nazareth's earthly experience but is open to each person
who is willing to be united to him in his own, unrepeatable
experience. Christ then absorbs it, makes it his own without taking anything from it or the person except the "nothingness" of its evil, just as the victim soul's participation in his life
comes about in a radical way.[17]

And from the darkness of her tunnel,

> "she made the Gospel shine appealingly in our time; she
> helped to heal souls of the rigours and fears of Jansenism
> which tended to stress God's justice rather than his divine
> mercy. In God's mercy she contemplated and adored all
> the divine perfections, because 'even his justice (and per-
> haps even more so than the other perfections) seems to me

clothed in love' [Ms A, 83v]. Thus she became a living icon of that God who, according to the Church's prayer, 'shows his almighty power in his mercy and forgiveness [cf. *Roman Missal*, Opening prayer, 26th Sunday in Ordinary Time]."[18]

St. Thérèse writes:

May Jesus pardon me if I have caused Him any pain, but He knows very well that while I do not have *the joy of faith*, I am trying to carry out its works at least. I believe I have made more acts of faith in this past year than all through my whole life. At each new occasion of combat, when my enemies provoke me, I conduct myself bravely. Knowing it is cowardly to enter into a duel, I turn my back on my adversaries without deigning to look them in the face; but I run toward my Jesus. I tell him I am ready to shed my blood to the last drop to profess my faith in the existence of *heaven*. I tell him, too, I am happy not to enjoy this beautiful heaven on earth so that He will open it for all eternity to poor unbelievers. Also, in spite of this trial which has taken away *all my joy*, I can nevertheless cry out: "*You have given me DELIGHT, O Lord, in ALL your doings*" [Ps. 91:5]. For is there a *joy* greater than that of suffering out of love for You?"[19]

Knowing through loving

Exercising the theological virtues, St. Thérèse or any believer, for that matter, can say "I have not yet won, but am still running, trying to capture the prize to which God calls us upwards to receive in Christ Jesus" (Phil 3:13). This sums up the reason for St. Thérèse's unfailing hope and her striving after a beatitude not yet possessed by her or her entrusted souls. In other words, she and her souls find themselves in a sort of *status viatoris* or state of journeying as opposed to the blessed who are in a *status comprehensoris* or state of realization. This lack of fulfilment, this "not yet" aspect of earthly Christian life refers more to an incomplete being than an incomplete journey—absence of fulfilment and nonetheless, orientation towards fulfilment. Since our being is not yet fulfilled, we are on pilgrimage and in perpetual journeying unto death and fulfilment.

This fundamental relationship between the state of grace and the act of being in the life of a journeying Christian can be appreciated by their necessary interdependence. For fundamental to and constitutive of the negative side of this journeying state is being on the brink of nothingness. That is the very nature of creatures because to have been created, they had to come from nothing. This is apparent in the choices made in life: there are those that fulfil being (morally good acts) and those that lead to nothingness (sin), a turning to the frustration of non-being.

Being and nothing are not equal choices and the abyss that separates them escapes all imagining. Thus teetering in this life between fulfilled existence and radical non-fulfilment, the journeying Christian, aware of what is at stake discovers—often to his own shock and bewilderment—that he is not equipped to bring about his own realization. God supplies the necessary means under the guise of faith, hope, and love. The theological virtues are the only antidote to this nihilist despair of "not yet."[20]

One finds an apparent, initial convergence between Nietzsche and St. Thérèse of Lisieux, who both maintain that if God does not exist, then nothing really matters. But here the

similarity ends. Although Nietzsche was referring to axio-
logical judgments, our Carmelite makes her claim universal:
"May I never seek nor find anything but Yourself alone. May
creatures be nothing for me and may I be nothing for them.
But may You, Jesus, be *everything!*"[21] If God exists, nothing
is unimportant; hence the genesis of Thérèse's renowned
"Little Way."

Whereas Nietzsche denied the ability to know and attain
God, St. Thérèse says that we indeed can know God, albeit
not through the intellect, but through the science of love.[22] We
attain God by becoming children (Mt. 18:3),[23] for "it is to such
as these little ones that the kingdom of heaven belongs" (Mk.
10:14). It is not until one opens one's heart to God, allowing
him free access and freedom of movement through self-donation that one really begins to know him.[24] And living in this
habitual attitude of mutual self-giving between the believer
and Creator, everything becomes important as its transcendence is revealed in him. In other words, rather than by way
of transfer of intellectual data, knowledge of God is obtained
through love. For the love of Christ embraces the entire truth
of Christ, "until knowing the love of Christ, which is beyond
all knowledge, you are filled with the utter fullness of God"
(Eph. 3:19). Therefore, St. Thérèse's doctrine, much the same
as the Gospel, does not permit a dichotomy of conviction and
act, between personal identity and mission. All of St. Thérèse's
actions will be caught up in this single act of self-giving to
her Beloved. If her mission in the Church is going to be love,
then this begins in her loving Christ who is love (1 Jn. 4:7-8).[25]
Thérèse's life will be dedicated to loving God in the smallest of details of her daily responsibilities, making a conscious

oblation of everything. This is loving and, thereby, knowing God experientially.

Therefore, St. Thérèse is not ashamed to remain in what Nietzsche would pejoratively call "the infant stage of religion." In fact, this is her goal. *Scientia amoris* requires such child-like simplicity if it is to find echo in a soul. She comes to understand that God has entrusted her with the mission of making known the way of littleness as the convergence of the way to God, sanctification, and the salvation of souls in one loving act.

The freedom of obedience

Nietzsche proclaimed God's death and St. Thérèse finishes this cry with "but he is risen" with her firm confidence in him even in her darkest moments and temptations to disbelief. And it is precisely submission and obedience to God dead on a cross that purchases true freedom. As the concept of freedom moved Nietzsche to jettison everything else in order to possess it, St. Thérèse was ardently moved to lose her freedom in her "desire to become a prisoner in exchange for souls captive of sin"[26] as she relates before her entrance into Carmel. Nonetheless, in a turn of the same image, she considers the special permission to enter the convent at a young age the result of her pleading to "Jesus to break my bonds."[27] Rather than careless use of imagery or a contradiction, Thérèse points to authentic freedom found only in unconditional abandonment to Christ the Truth which sets her free (cf. Jn. 8:32). Becoming his prisoner does not imply frustration of one's will, but realization of God's will which liberates the soul to act with the greatest degree of liberty: freedom for perfection.

In other words, rather than a dialectic of repression, empty self-renunciation, or senseless abandonment versus Nietzsche's Dionysian abandonment of self to one's passions, St. Thérèse of the Child Jesus' self-oblation is the free use of her will which binds her definitively to her Divine Spouse and assures eternal freedom for her and the souls entrusted to her.

Her sacrifices were not offered up from the ivory tower of the cloister, in a condescending act of pity for sinners. Rather, God allowed her to experience their darkness of faith, to participate in their temptations,[28] loneliness and distance experienced by souls who have rejected God:

> "If you only knew what frightful thoughts obsess me! Pray very much for me in order that I do not listen to the devil who wants to persuade me about so many lies. It's the reasoning of the worst materialists which is imposed upon my mind: Later, unceasingly make new advances, science will explain everything naturally; we shall have the absolute reason for everything that exists and that still remains a problem, because there remain very many things to be discovered, etc., etc. I want to do good after my death, but I will not be able to do so! It will be as it was for Mother Geneviéve: We expected to see her work miracles, and complete silence fell over her tomb . . . "Finally I offer up these very great pains to obtain the light of faith for poor unbelievers, for all those who separate themselves from the Church's beliefs."[29]

To only the humble is it given to hope

From Easter 1896 until her death from tuberculosis on September 30, 1897, at age twenty-four, Thérèse's existence was akin to being trapped within a dark tunnel. She suffered this interior turmoil without weakening, without revisiting her reasons for believing, for her faith was not fruit of feelings or circumstances, but of conviction of the truth of Christ joined to her will to believe.

St. Thérèse also manifested a holy indifference before the sacrifices demanded of her. Her peace was found in her internal and spiritual sacrifices[30] rather than her external mortifications. Nonetheless, she frequently seeks out such corporal penance even in a fevered state, denying herself water when dehydrated,[31] and makes the ultimate sacrifice of all which is to abandon herself to the Holy Spirit so that he choose whatever sacrifice is needed in order to spread God's mercy and make reparation.[32]

From the moment she first embarks upon this apostolate of atonement and intercession—that fight for the soul of Pranzini—Thérèse manifests a surety and confidence which has confounded some of her biographers. Rather than what has been misconstrued as presumption, she exercises a child-like, all-encompassing trust in the goodness of her heavenly Father. In fact, St. Faustina similarly writes in her diary that "confidence is the key to Divine Mercy."[33] In other words, St. Thérèse's trust is not foremost in her ability to move the divine will, but in her intimate understanding of the utter goodness and mercy of the divine will which desires her humble and frequent supplications. St. Thérèse is merely fulfilling Christ's mandate to pray constantly and confidently (cf. Lk. 18:1–8) as well as humbly (cf. Lk. 18:9–14). Justice and mercy balance each other as hope balances the soul. Hence there can be no quarter for despair or presumption, for the despairing cannot pray, and the presumptuous petition falsely. As far as St. Thérèse in concerned, God cannot fail her.

This confidence amid her trial of faith was theologically well founded. She always expresses the evils she endures as God's permission of evil, rather than rooted in punishment or his indifferent transcendence.[34] Such was St. Thérèse's confidence in God, as well as in the divine nature of her vocation that, when asked if she has had or would want to have supernatural visions, she replied that she prefers the darkness of faith to its consolations and even visions, were they permitted her by God because she, like Job, knew her Redeemer lives.

Further, there is a certain logic to exercising such adamant confidence in one's apostolate. If it is God's will that one carry it out, if it was his initiative and one is simply obeying lovingly, certainly God obliges himself to make it fruitful. This yielding of one's will to God's is the key to unyielding hope. "Only to the humble is it given to hope."[35]

This aspect did not escape the Holy Father's notice as he wrote "although a cloistered and hidden nun, her life possesses a mysterious fruitfulness for spreading the Gospel and the fills the Church and the world with the sweet odour of Christ [cf. LT 169, 2v.]."[36]

Nonetheless, one must not underestimate the intensity of her trials even as she trusted. Her faith and confidence were maintained only with valiant struggle[37] and moved by heroic charity. Disconsolate in her Job-like trials (Job 13:15),[38] she offers it all up so that no one else have to endure what she suffers.[39]

*More than that, we rejoice in our sufferings, knowing
that suffering produces endurance, and endurance
produces character, and character produces hope, and
hope does not disappoint us, because God's love has been
poured into our hearts through the Holy Spirit which
has been given to us.*

—*Rom. 5:3–5*

Conclusion

St. Thérèse had implacable confidence in her Beloved and this made her eminently solution oriented. For her, darkness and suffering were useful means and not the inescapable destiny of nihilism. As love ignites ingenuity and illumines the lover how better to love the beloved, St. Thérèse saw her chance in her trial and used it for all it was worth, thus winning for herself and countless other souls, "the wreath that will never wither" (1 Cor. 9:25).

This nun once, hidden behind cloistered walls and now hidden from us in Heaven, continues to teach us:

"Our time, perhaps more than any other, seeks living witnesses and clear teachers of the truth. But the example of the witnesses is necessary first to give credence to words. St. Thérèse of Lisieux, aware that her mission would truly begin after her death, established the credibility of her words with a heroic life of love and hope. For this reason she is also loved and accepted by brothers and sisters of other Christian communities and even by non-Christians."[1]

She is a universal teacher, a Doctor of the Church who is quoted 6 times in the *Catechism of the Catholic Church*, Co-Patroness of Missionaries, and friendly helper to millions who call upon her assistance. Her simple and gruelling life was lived on a supernatural level open to all but experienced only by the saints. This permitted her to penetrate the superficiality of the one dimensional *scientia intellecti* (natural science) of her age, going beyond the tangible and confronting evil at its roots. For beyond mere pain and in the heart of each man, at depths that neither science nor medicine can reach, where the evil of suffering is rooted, Christ does battle for the soul. To those dark passages St. Thérèse "went down as a bride adorned for husband" (cf. Rev. 21:2) and joined in the fray.

There, although hidden from her vision, was her Beloved.

St. Thérèse of Lisieux continues to serve as an example. But much more than that, she is present as a fellow warrior in our own dark struggles, helping us to have the same awareness of the eternal transcendence of each moment. The proof of her heroic faith, hope, and charity was her self-offering as a victim to save atheists. The fact that she lived up to this ideal with perfection is proof that it is also possible for us. Nonetheless, we should bear in mind what she quickly added after making her offering:

"offering oneself as a victim is not enough. Words are ineffective! To be a real victim of love one has to offer oneself totally. In as much as we are consumed by his love and in as much as we immolate ourselves for his love."[2] There, and later in Heaven, St. Thérèse proved that "Jesus' promises are fulfilled in the believer who knows how confidently to welcome in his own life the saving presence of the Redeemer."[3]

Appendix

Thérèse's Self-Offering as Holocaust

J.M.J.T.

Offering of myself as a victim of Holocaust to God's Merciful Love

O My God! Most Blessed Trinity, I desire to *Love* You and make You *Loved*, to work for the glory of Holy Church by saving souls on earth and liberating those suffering in purgatory. I desire to accomplish Your will perfectly and to reach the degree of glory You have prepared for me in Your Kingdom. I desire, in a word, to be a saint, but I feel my helplessness and I beg You, O my God! to be Yourself my *Sanctity*!

Since You loved me so much as to give me Your only Son as my Savior and my Spouse, the infinite treasures of His merits are mine. I offer them to You with gladness, begging You to look upon me only in the Face of Jesus and in His heart burning with *Love*.

I offer You, too, all the merits of the saints (in heaven and on earth), their acts of *Love*, and those of the holy angels. Finally, I offer You, *O Blessed Trinity!* the *Love* and merits of the *Blessed Virgin, my dear Mother*. It is to her I abandon my offering, begging her to present it to You. Her Divine Son, my *Beloved Spouse*, told us in the days of His mortal life: *"Whatsoever you ask the Father in my name he will give it to you!"* I am certain, then, that You will grant my desires; I know, O my

God! that *the more You want to give, the more You make us desire.* I feel in my heart immense desires and it is with confidence I ask You to come and take possession of my soul. Ah! I cannot receive Holy Communion as often as I desire, but, Lord, are You not *all-powerful*? Remain in me as in a tabernacle and never separate Yourself from Your little victim.

I want to console You for the ingratitude of the wicked, and I beg of You to take away my freedom to displease You. If through weakness I sometimes fall, may Your *Divine Glance* cleanse my soul immediately, consuming all my imperfections like the fire that transforms everything into itself.

I thank You, O my God! for all the graces You have granted me, especially the grace of making me pass through the crucible of suffering. It is with joy I shall contemplate You on the Last Day carrying the sceptre of Your Cross. Since You deigned to give me a share in this very precious Cross, I hope in heaven to resemble You and to see shining in my glorified body the sacred stigmata of Your Passion.

After earth's Exile, I hope to go and enjoy You in the Fatherland, but I do not want to lay up merits for heaven. I want to work for Your *Love alone* with the one purpose of pleasing You, consoling Your Sacred Heart, and saving souls who will love You eternally.

In the evening of this life, I shall appear before You with empty hands, for I do not ask You, Lord, to count my works. All our justice is stained in Your eyes. I wish, then, to be clothed in Your own *Justice* and to receive from Your *Love* the eternal possession of *Yourself*. I want no other *Throne*, no other *Crown* but *You*, my *Beloved*!

Time is nothing in Your eyes, and a single day is like a thousand years. You can, then, in one instant prepare me to appear before You.

In order to live in one single act of perfect Love, I OFFER MYSELF AS A VICTIM OF HOLOCAUST TO YOUR MERCIFUL LOVE, asking You to consume me incessantly, allowing the waves of *infinite tenderness* shut up within You to overflow into my soul, and that thus I may become a *martyr* of Your *Love*, O my God!

May this martyrdom, after having prepared me to appear before You, finally cause me to die and may my soul take its flight without any delay into the eternal embrace of *Your Merciful Love.*

I want, O my *Beloved*, at each beat of my heart to renew this offering to You an infinite number of times, until the shadows having disappeared I may be able to tell You of my *Love* in an *Eternal Face to Face!*

Marie, Francoise, Thérèse of the Child Jesus
and the Holy Face, unworthy Carmelite religious.

This 9th day of June,
Feast of the Most Holy Trinity,
In the year of grace, 1895.

Thérèse' Wedding Invitation

"God Almighty, Creator of Heaven and Earth, Sovereign Ruler of the Universe, and the Glorious Virgin Mary, Queen of the Heavenly Court, announce to you the Spiritual Espousals of their August Son, Jesus, King of Kings and Lord of Lords, with little Thérèse Martin, now Princess and Lady of His Kingdoms of the Holy Childhood and the Passion, assigned to her as a dowry, by her Divine Spouse, from which Kingdoms she holds her titles of nobility—of the Child Jesus and of the Holy Face.

It was not possible to invite you to the Nuptial Blessing which took place on the Mountain of Carmel, September 8, 1890 (the Heavenly Court was alone admitted), but you are requested to be present at the Return from the Wedding which will take place Tomorrow, the day of Eternity, when Jesus, the Son of God, will come in the Clouds of Heaven, in the splendor of His Majesty, to judge the Living and the Dead.

"The hour being still uncertain, you are asked to hold yourselves in readiness and watch."

Notes

Introduction

1 *Story of a Soul—The Autobiography of St. Thérèse of Lisieux*, ICS Publications: Washington, DC, 1996. Ms A, 45r. *Hereafter, *Story of a Soul* (SS) will be referred to by the corresponding manuscript or SS for those citations taken from the epilogue.

2 Ibid.

3 Ibid.

4 THOMAS AQUINAS: most influential philosopher, theologian, and Doctor of the Church. Called the Angelic Doctor. Died in 1274.

5 THOMAS AQUINAS, *In symbolum apostolorum*, 1,i citing Hosea 2:20. Interestingly, John Paul II presents the theological virtues in their nuptial function in *Dominum et Vivificantem*, n. 51: "faith, in its deepest essence, is the openness of the human heart to the gift: to God's self-communication in the Holy Spirit." This life which is poured out for Christ's Bride as he died on the Cross is the Holy Spirit whose sign of life in the individual person takes the form of the theological virtues.

6 Cf. *Novo Millennio Inuente*, 27.

Chapter 1

1 Sr. Thérèse is writing at the behest of her sister Pauline (Mother Agnes of Jesus, OCD) who had become her superior in religious life.

2 Ms A, 4v.

3 Ms A, 28v. "I believe the devil had received an external power over me but [A, 29r.] was not allowed to approach my soul nor my mind except to inspire me with very great fears of certain things. I was absolutely terrified by everything: my

bed seemed to be surrounded by frightful precipices; some nails in the wall of the room took on the appearance of big black charred fingers, making me cry out in fear. One day, while Papa was looking at me in silence, the hat in his hand was suddenly transformed into some indescribable dreadful shape, and I showed such great fear that poor Papa left the room sobbing."

4   P. AHERN, *Maurice & Thérèse: The Story of a Love*, Darton, Longman, and Todd, London: 1999, p. 174.

5   T. TAYLOR, *St.Thérèse of Lisieux, the Little Flower of Jesus*, P.J. Kennedy, New York: 1926, p. 125.

6   Ms A, 26r.

7   Ibid.

8   Ms A, 69v.

9   Ms A, 73r.

10 Ms A, 76v.

Chapter 2

1   For PR, P, Pr, and L, I use *Obras Completas de Santa Teresa de Liseieux, Centenaria Edición*, Folioviews Edition, 1994.

2   Ms C, 36r.

3   "The science of love," Thérèse's adopted term taken from John of the Cross.

4   *Novo Millennio Ineunte*, 44.

5   BERNARD OF CLAIRVAUX, Born in 1090, at Fontaines, near Dijon, France, died on, 21 August, 1153 at Clairvaux. Co-Founder of the Cistercians and founder of countless monasteries.

6   *NMI*, 27.

7   Ibid., 41.

8   JOHN PAUL II, *Divini Amoris Scientia: Saint Thérèse of the Child Jesus Proclaimed a Doctor of the Universal Church*, no. 1.

9 *NMI*, 27.

10 Cfr. *The Dialogue*. Suzanne Noffke, OP (trans.), Paulist Press, New York: 1980, No. 78, p. and Letter No. 273 compared with Thérèse of Lisieux, LC 6, July, 1897.

11 CATHERINE OF SIENA: Third Order Dominican, hermit, reformer, mystic, d. 1380.

12 John Paul II says that "holiness is measured according to the 'great mystery' in which the Bride responds with the gift of love to the gift of the Bridegroom." *Mulieris Dignitatem*, n. 27. Love Incarnate being loved by his earthly spouse reciprocates, thus effecting a reconciliation of divinity and humanity. Brides of Christ apply the fruits of this love and reconciliation to their entrusted souls.

13 Ms A, 2v.

14 *DAS*, 1

15 Ms C, 36r–v.

16 PSEUDO-DIONYSIUS: c. end of the 5th Cent.–1st half of the 6th Cent. spiritual writer.

17 *De Nominibus Dei*, 680 D, 68–69. (trans. John D. Jones), Marquette University Press, Milwaukee, 1980, p. 283.

18 Ms A, 2v.

19 Ms B, 1r.

Chapter 3

1 AA. VV. *Dizionario di Mistica*. Libreria Editrice Vaticana, Città di Vaticano, 1998, p. 1277.

2 Vol. IV, (trans. M.F. Taol), D.D., Henry Regnery Co, Chicago: 1964, p. 221.

3 P, 35, 8.

4 P, 3, 6.

5 Cf. Ms A, 37r–37v.

6 *DAS*, 9.

7 Ms A, 52vr.
8 Ms A, 53r.
9 Ms A, 2v.
10 Ms A, 6v.
11 Ms A, 26r.
12 Ms A, 21r.
13 Ms A, 30r–30v.
14 Ms A, 40r.
15 Ms A, 35r.
16 Ms A, 3v.
17 Ms A, 70r.

Chapter 4

1 H. SCHLIER, *Nur aber Bleiben diese Drei. Grundriss des Christlichen Lebensvollzuges*, Einsiedln 1971, p. 12.
2 Cfr. II Pet. 1:4.
3 *S. Th.* III, 62, Ic.
4 *S. Th.* Ia I, 8 ad 2um.
5 *S Th.* I–IIae, 113, 10.
6 *S.Th.* II–Iiae, 2, 2 ad 1um.
7 *Discourses to Mixed Congregations*, "Faith and Doubt," Oxford University Press: London: 1881, p. 216.
8 AMBROSE, *Secunda Epistula ad Valentianum*, PL 16, *Lib*. X, 73, 1015, p. 38.
9 *Oxford University Sermons*, "Love the Safeguard of Faith against Superstition," Oxford University Press, London, 1880, p. 236.
10 Ms A, 45r–45v
11 Ms A, 44v–45v.
12 Ms. A, 45v.
13 Ms A, 46v.
14 Ms A, 46r.
15 Ms A, 46r.

16 Ms A, 47r.
17 Ms A, 44v.
18 Ms A, 68v.
19 Ibid.
20 Ms B, 1r.
21 P 45, 7.
22 L 122.
23 P 45, 7.
24 P 24, 31.
25 II–IIae, q. 27 art. 4, 5 and 6.
26 L 74.
27 II–IIae, q. 24 art. 7.

Chapter 5

1 Cfr. 1 Pet. 1:12.
2 Ms A, 69r.
3 Ms A, 69v.
4 Ibid.
5 *St. Thérèse of Lisieux by Those Who Knew Her: Testimonies from the Process of Beatification*, (ed. and trans. by Christopher O'Mahoney, OCD), Our Sunday Visitor, inc.: Huntington, In. 1975, p. 63.
6 Ms 71r.
7 *St. Thérèse of Lisieux by those who knew her. Op. cit.*
8 Ms A, 70v.

Chapter 6

1 Cfr. Jer. 2:20; Ez. 16:33, ff.; Hosea 2; the entire book of Canticle of Canticles.
2 Cfr. Mt. 9:15; 22:2; 26:1–13; Lk. 12:36; Rev. 19:7–10; 21:3
3 TERTULLIAN: Ecclesiastical writer in the second and third centuries, b. probably about 160 at Carthage.

4 "The flesh follows the soul which is now married to the spirit, as part of the bridal offering, no longer servant of the soul but of the spirit." De Anima PL 2, 720.

5 *Omilie in genesim*, PG 12, 218.

6 CYRILL of JERUSALEM: Bishop of Jerusalem and Doctor of the Church, born about 315; died probably 18 March, 386.

7 *De baptismo*. PL 2, 720.

8 DIDYMUS the BLIND: learned layman, of Alexandria, b. about 310 or 313; d. about 395 or 398.

9 *De trinitate*, PG 34, 692 A.

10 ORIGEN: one of the most influential patristic writers, b. in Alexandria in 185, d. in 232.

11 GREGORY of NYSSA: Date of birth unknown; died after 385 or 386. He belongs to the group known as the "Cappadocian Fathers," a title which reveals at once his birthplace in Asia Minor and his intellectual characteristics.

12 Vol. IV, 83,3. p.182.

13 *Op. cit.* 82,8. p.179.

14 III, 24. *The Collected Works of St. John of the Cross*, ICS, Wash. DC. 1973, p. 619.

15 Ibid.

16 Biblioteca de Autores Cristianos, Madrid: 1985, p. 737.

17 SS, p. 275.

18 Ms B, 3v.

19 SS, p. 275.

20 L, 2, 219, 220, 221; PR 8; LC, p. 217.

21 Ms B, 2v.

22 Ms A, 57r.

23 Ms A, 83v.

24 LC, p. 55.

25 Ms B, 2v.

26 Ms B, 3v.

27 Ms B, 5r.

28 Ms C, 5v – 7v.

29 Ms A, 80v.

30 Ms A, 84r.

31 "Shortly after Thérèse's death, her sister Pauline (by this time Mother Agnes, superior of the community), convinced that Thérèse was a saint, decided to edit all the manuscripts concerning Thérèse to ensure nothing indiscreet would see the light of day. She proceeded to delete, condense, expand, interpolate, and reorganize at will." Philip Zaleski, "The Love of Thérèse," First Things, New York: Vol. 9, December, 2004, p 21.

32 LC, p 140.

Chapter 7

1 *Catechism of the Catholic Church*, 1849.

2 Ibid., 1850.

3 *De rationibus Fidei*, Q.2., art. 3.

4 *Mystici Corporis*, 12.

5 Ibid., 16.

6 Ms A, 83v.

7 Pr 2.

Chapter 8

1 *NMI*, 27.

2 Cf. *S. Th.* I – IIae, 103, 3.

3 Cf. Book III, 33 – 35.

4 *Dialogue*, (trans. Suzanne Noffke, OP), Paulist Press, New York: 1980, p. 223.

5 "To call oneself 'victim' is easy and pleases self-love; but to make oneself a victim demands such a purity, a detachment from creatures, a heroism abandoned to every type of suffering, to every type of humiliation, and such unexpected and ineffable darkness, that I would call it either crazy or

miraculous that in the beginnings of one's spiritual life, he should attempt to do what the divine Master only did by progression." Mother María Teresa of the Heart of Jesus, Foundress of the Adoración Repardora whose life ended in flames, a literal holocaust offering. Cited in *Cristo nei Nostri Fratelli*, by R. Plus, Marietti, Roma: 1934, p. 178.

6 Ms A, 71v. The concept of formally offering oneself as a victim and holocaust was brought to France by the Frenchman Cardinal Bérulle in the early 17th Century. He was initiated into this spirituality during his time in Spain. For him, the Incarnation was the beginning of all spirituality, and the path to holiness lay in its imitation. Such imitation requires a permanent disposition more than the exteriors of Christ's earthly life. He tried to impose the act of self-offering as a fourth vow for Carmelites, which met with disastrous consequences. Montfort's concept of "slave of Divine Love" shows him to be a faithful Berullian who translates Bérulle into simple language much as St. Thérèse of Lisieux translates St. John of the Cross into easily accessible terms. The Carmelite convent at Lisieux was a Bérullian convent in an age in which Jansenist tendencies had deformed the self offering by highlighting God's punishment.

Chapter 9

1 *NMI*, 41.

2 LC, p. 225.

3 Ms B, 3v.

4 Ms B4v

5 Ms B, 5v.

6 *The Drama of Atheistic Humanism*, Ignatius Press, San Francisco: 1995, p.14. See Oliver O'Donavan's fine book on this subject, *The Desire of the Nations: Rediscovering the Roots of*

Political Theology (New York: Cambridge University Press, 1999), p. 49, where he says that "the nature of the impasse into which a politics constructed in an avowedly anti-sacred basis has now come. For without the act of worship political authority is unbelievable, so that the binding political loyalties and obligations seem to be deprived of any point. The doctrine that we set up political authority, as a device to secure our own essentially private, local and unpolitical purposes, has left the Western democracies in a state of pervasive moral debilitation, which, from time to time, inevitably throws up idolatrous and authoritarian reactions."

7 Ms A, 84r.
8 Ibid.
9 "Act of Oblation of Merciful Love," SS, pp. 276–277.
10 Ms C, 35v.
11 Ibid.
12 Ms C, 34r.
13 Cf. Rom. 5:20. "My grace is enough for you."
14 L, 17 Sept. '96.
15 LC, p. 145.
16 Ms C, 5r.
17 *SD* 26.
18 *SD 9.*
19 SS, "Act of Oblation to Merciful Love," pp. 276–277.

Chapter 10

1 See Carol Zaleski, *"The Dark Night of Mother Teresa,"* First Things, New York: May, 2003, No. 133, p. 25.
2 Ms C, 5v.
3 "Who would have suspected, except for the few who actually knew, that during this time Thérèse remained constantly

"in the night," in that "undergound passage," "before that impenetrable wall." SS, p. 266.

4 He presents God through the attribute of Goodness. God as source and centre of all creation reflects his goodness through this visible effect.

5 WILLIAM OF THIERRY: 1075/80–1148. One of the greatest Medieval spiritual writers whose mission was to reform the Church via the reformation of monastic life. His effort to restore and renew monastic spiritual and disciplinary life was in tandem with St. Bernard of Clairvaux's work. In words as simple as they are profound he gives a valid definition of Thérèse's *scientia amoris*: "Love of God is understanding Him: He is not known unless He is loved, nor is He loved unless He is known; and in reality He is known only to the degree that He is loved, and loved to the degree that He is known." Expositio in Cant., c I:ML 180, 499,c.

6 JANE FRANCES DE CHANTEL: 1572–1641 Co-Foundress of the Visitation Order along with St. Francis de Sales.

7 PAUL OF THE CROSS: 1697–1775. Founder of the Passionists.

8 JOHN OF THE CROSS: 1542–1591. Reformer of the Carmelites.

9 PIO DI PIETRELCINA: 1882–1968. Capuchin priest, stigmatist, and "humble friar who prays."

10 TERESA OF CALCUTTA: 1910–1997. Foundress of the Missionaries of Charity.

11 In the *Ascent of Mount Carmel*, I: 2,2, St. John of the Cross explains how the exercise of the theological virtues blinds Satan and protects the soul from his attacks as it purifies the faculties of the intellect (faith), will (charity), and memory (hope).

12 Ms C, 6v.

13 LC, pp. 223–224.

14 J.H. NEWMAN, *The Oxford Sermons: Faith and Reason*, Christian Classics: Westminster, Md. p. 198.

15 NIETZSCHE, Friedrich Wilhelm (1844–1900). German philosopher and poet, one of the most original and influential figures in modern philosophy. As one of the fathers of nihilism, Nietzsche posits the will to power and the abandonment to one's passions as the way to self-realization.

16 Cf. S. PINCKAERS, OP, *Sources of Christian Ethics*, T&T Clarke, Edinburgh, 1995, p. 43.

17 COMTE, Auguste Marie (1789–1857) French-born father of positivism. He divided human history into three periods: the religious age (childhood), the Metaphysical age (youth), the Positivistic age (full adulthood). He predicted that this last epoch, marked by the claim that all truth is accessible and verifiable through the senses, would be elevated to a world religion of humanism by 1860. Although this thought boasts some adherents today, it still has not been able to demonstrate itself through the senses.

18 See *The Drama of Atheist Humanism*, pp. 42–58.

19 "Ein Mensch der will befiehlt einem Etwas in sich, dass gehorcht oder von dem er glaubt, dass es gehorcht." (To will is to command obedience, or at the least apparent obedience) *Jenseits von Gut und Böse*, No. 9. in *Friedrich Nietzsches Kritische Gesamtausgabe*, Wolfgang Rothe Verlag, Heidelberg: 1961, p. 159.

20 The Three Ages of the Interior Life: Prelude of Eternal Life, Vol. II, trans. Sr. M. Timothea Doyle, O.P. Tan Books and Publishers, Inc. Rockford, Il. 1989, p. 437.

21 *Soeur Thérèse Of Lisieux, The Little Flower of Jesus*. Burns & Oates, Ltd, 1912, pp. 227–228. *Sainte Thérèse de lEnfant Jésus Histoire D'Une Ame, "Souvenirs et Conseils,"* p. 263–264.

Chapter 11

1   *Amén* in Hebrew means "to stand firm," "to believe," "to entrust oneself," "to abandon oneself to another," "to be established" and the Hellenistic influence in later Judaism gave it a new usage implying "to understand." J. Ratzinger, *Introduction to Christianity*, Ignatius Press, San Francisco: 2004, pp. 69–74.

2   *Friedrich Nietzsches Kritische Gesamtausgabe*, Wolfgang Rothe Verlag, Heidelberg: 1961, p. 321.

3   A. SICARI, *Retratos de Santos*, Madrid: Ediciones Encuentros, 1996, p. 140.

4   The Three Ages of the Interior Life: Prelude of Eternal Life, Vol. II, trans. Sr. M. Timothea Doyle, O.P. Tan Books and Publishers, Inc. Rockford, Il. 1989, p. 504.

5   *NMI*, 27.

6   Book I, 9:2,3,9.

7   Cf. L 247 in which St. Thérèse says clearly that she took this austere road, not in purgation of her own sins, but as expiation for sinners.

8   Ms A, 70r.

9   Ms C, 6v.

10   The Three Ages of the Interior Life: Prelude of Eternal Life, Vol. II, trans. Sr. M. Timothea Doyle, O.P. Tan Books and Publishers, Inc. Rockford, Il. 1989, p. 508–509.

11   Ms C, 5v.

12   Ms C, 6r.

13   *DAS*, 11.

14   *Dialogue*, p. 273.

15   Garrigou-Lagrange, *op. cit.*

16   *Saint Thérèse of Lisieux: The Little Flower of Jesus*, trans. Rev. Thomas N. Taylor (NY: P.J. Kennedy and Sons, 1927), p. 205.

17   Cf. *SD* 24.

18 *DAS*, 8.

19 Ms C, 7r.

20 Cf. J. PIEPER, *Faith, Hope Love*, Ignatius Press, San Francisco, 1997, p. 96–98.

21 SS, "A Letter Sister Thérèse Carried on Her Heart on the Day of Her Profession" September 8, 1890. p. 275.

22 "The science of love, ah, yes, this word resounds sweetly in the ear of my soul, and I desire only this science. Having given all my riches for it, I esteem it as having given nothing as did the bride in the Sacred Canticles. I understand so well that it is only love that makes us acceptable to God, that this love is the only good I ambition." Ms B, 1r.

23 "I tell you solemnly, unless you change and become like little children you will never enter the kingdom of heaven."

24 According to the Holy Father's Letter *Divini amoris scientia*, 1, the gift of *scientia amoris* is "only granted to the little and humble so that they may know and proclaim the secrets of the kingdom, hidden from the learned and the wise; for this reason Jesus rejoiced in the Holy Spirit, praising the Father who graciously willed it so (cf. Lk. 10:21–22; Mt. 11: 25–26)." Ms A, 83v; Ms B, 1r; Ms C, 36r all treat of St. Thérèse's meta-logical knowledge and how it was through contemplation that she learned directly from her Divine Teacher the mysteries of the kingdom. The Holy Father affirms that this was one of St. Thérèse's particular charisms.

25 "My dear children, let us love one another since love comes from God and everyone who loves is begotten by God and knows God. Anyone who fails to love can never have known God, because God is love."

26 Ms A, 67r.

27 Ibid.

28 Ms C, 7v: St. Thérèse encounters an almost personal knowledge of blasphemy and incredulity. Nonetheless, her response "I want to believe!" a perfect act of faith, is the only adequate response.

29 LC, pp. 257–258.

30 LC, p. 160

31 Ibid., p. 264.

32 Ibid., p. 240.

33 KOWALSKA, F., *Divine Mercy in My Soul*, Marian Press, Stockbridge, Ma. 2004, Notebook III, 1074.

34 "He permitted my soul to be invaded by the thickest darkness and that the thought of heaven, up until then so sweet to me, be no longer anything but the cause of struggle and torment." Ms C, 5v. "I believe the demon has asked God permission to tempt me with an extreme suffering, to make me fail in patience and faith." *Last Conversations*, p. 168. Her temptation is against the existence of Heaven or at least it being open to her. Certainly, such a trial must have been excruciating for a soul consecrated to God and to sacrificing for the salvation of sinners.

35 AUGUSTINE, *Comm. Ps*, 118, 15,2. in, *Nicene and Post-Nicene Fathers, Vol. 8*, Phillip Schaff, (ed.), Online Ed. 2004.

36 *DAS*, 11.

37 LC, Aug. 6th, 1897.

38 "Even were he to take my life, I trust in him."

39 LC, June 5th, 1897.

Conclusion

1 *DAS*, 11.

2 LC, 33.

3 *DAS*, 10.

Bibliography

AA. VV., *Dizionario di Mistica*, Libreria Editrice Vaticana, Cittá di Vaticano, 1998.

Ahern, P., *Maurice & Thérèse: The Story of a Love*, Darton, Longman, and Todd, London: 1999.

Ambrose, *Opera Omnia*, CD-ROM, Folioviews ed.

Aquinas, T.

————. *Faith, Reason, and Theology*, University of Califorina Press, Berkely: Folioviews Edition, 1984.

————. *Summa Contra Gentiles*, ibid.

————. *Summa Theologiae*, ibid.

————. *Sunday Sermons of the Great Fathers*, Vol. IV, (trans. M.F. Taol), D.D.

————. *In Symbolum Apostolorum*, Folioviews Ed., 1984, Henry Regnery Co, Chicago: 1964.

Augustine, *Nicene and Post-Nicene Fathers,* Vol. 8, Phillip Schaff, (ed.), Online Ed. 2004.

Catherine of Siena, *The Dialogue*. Suzanne Noffke, OP (trans.), Paulist Press, New York: 1980.

Cyrill of Jerusalem, *Nicene and Post-Nicene Fathers*, Vol. I, 2nd series, K Knight, Online Edition. 2005.

Daniélou, J., *Bibbia e liturgia. La teologia biblica dei sacramenti e delle feste secondo i Padri della Chiesa*, Societá Editrice Vite e Pensiero, Milano: 1958.

De Lubac, H. *The Drama of Atheistic Humanism*, Ignatius Press, San Francisco: 1995.

————. *In Symbolum Apostolorum*, ibid.

GARRIGOU-LAGRANGE, OP, Reginald, The Three Ages of the Interior Life: Prelude of Eternal Life, Vol. II, trans. Sr. M. Timothea Doyle, O.P. Tan Books and Publishers, Inc. Rockford, Il.: 1989.

John of the Cross, *The Collected Works of St. John of the Cross*, (trans. Kieran Kavanaugh, OCD), Institute of Carmelite Studies, Wash. DC. 1973.

John Paul II, *Divinae Amoris Scientiae*

———. *Divini Amoris Scientiae*

———. *Dominum et Vivificantem*

———. *Mulieris Dignitatem*

———. *Novo Millennio Ineunte*

Kowalska, F., *Divine Mercy in My Soul*, Marian Press, Stockbridge, Ma.: 2004.

Marín, R., *La Teología de la Perfección Cristiana*, Biblioteca de Autores Cristianos, Madrid: 1985.

Martínez-Blat, Vicente, *Diccionario de Espiritualidad de anta Teresa, Edibesa, Madrdi*, 2003.

Newman, J.H., *Discourses to Mixed Congregations*, Oxford University Press, London: 1881.

———. *Oxford University Sermons*, Christian Classics, Westminster, Md., 1946.

Nietzsche, F. *Friedrich Nietzsches Kritische Gesamtausgabe*, Wolfgang Rothe Verlag, Heidelberg: 1961.

O'Donavan, O., *The Desire of the Nations: Rediscovering the Roots of Political Theology*, Cambridge University Press, New York: 1999.

O'Mahoney, C. (trans). *St. Thérèse of Lisieux by Those Who Knew Her: Testimonies from the Process of Beatification*, Our Sunday Visitor, inc. Huntington, In. 1975.

Origen, *Omelie sulla Genesi*, Cittá Nuova Editrice, Roma: 1978.

Pieper, J. *Faith, Hope, Love*, Ignatius Press, San Francisco, 1985.

Pinckaers, S. *Sources of Christian Ethics*, Ignatius Press, Sanfrancisco, 1995.

Pius XII, *Mystici Corporis*.

Plus, R. *Cristo nei Nostri Fratelli*, Marietti, Roma: 1934.

Pseudo-Dionysius, *De Nominibus Dei*, 680 D, 68–69, (trans. John D. Jones), Marquette University Press, Milwaukee, 1980.

Ratzinger, J., *Introduction to Christianity*, Ignatius Press, San Francisco: 2004,

Schlier, H., *Nur aber Bleiben diese Drei. Grundriss des Christlichen Lebensvollzuges*, Johannes Verlag, Einsiedln 1971.

Sicari, A., *Retratos de Santos*, Ediciones Encuentros, Madrid: 1996.

Taylor, T., *St.Thérèse of Lisieux, the Little Flower of Jesus*, P.J. Kennedy, New York: 1926.

Tertullian, *On the Soul*, Bk. II, chpt. 41, Online Ed. New Advent: 2004.

Thérèse of Lisieux, *Story of a Soul—The Autobiography of St. Thérèse of Lisieux*, (trans. John Clarke, OCD), ICS Publications: Washington, DC, 1996.

———. *Last Conversations*, ICS, Wash. D.C., 1977.

———. *Obras Completas, Edición del Centenario*, edición llevada a cabo por un equipo formado por sor Cecilia, del Carmelo de Lisieux, Mons. Guy Gaucher, OCD, obispo auxiliar de Bayeux y Lisieux, sor Genoveva, OP., y Jacques Lonchampt, con la colaboración del P. Bernard Bro, o.p., y de Jeanne Lonchampt. Folioviews Edition. 1992.

Zaleski, P., *The Love of Thérèse*, First Things, no. 153, New York: December, 2004.

Zaleski, C., *"The Dark Night of Mother Teresa,"* First Things, no. 133, New York: May, 2003.

The Institute of Carmelite Studies promotes research and publication in the field of Carmelite spirituality. Its members are Discalced Carmelites, part of a Roman Catholic community—friars, nuns, and laity—who are heirs to the teaching and way of life of Teresa of Jesus and John of the Cross, men and women dedicated to contemplation and to ministry in the Church and the world. Information concerning their way of life is available through local diocesan Vocation Offices or from the Vocation Directors' Offices:

1233 S. 45th Street, Milwaukee, WI 53214

1 Fallons Lane 1628 London, ON, Canada N6A 4C1

P.O. Box 3420, San Jose, CA 95156-3420

5151 Marylake Drive, Little Rock, AR 72206